Stitch
with
Love

Mandy Shaw

David and Charles

www.rucraft.co.uk

Dedication

To all those wonderful mums out there who teach their
kids to sew – I am so pleased my lovely mum taught me.

The author and publisher have made every effort to ensure that all
the instructions in the book are accurate and safe, and therefore
cannot accept liability for any resulting injury, damage or loss to
persons or property, however it may arise.
Names of manufacturers, fabric ranges and other products are
provided for the information of readers, with no intention to infringe
copyright or trademarks.

A catalogue record for this book is available from the British Library.

ISBN-13: 978-0-7153-3849-0 paperback
ISBN-10: 0-7153-3849-8 paperback

Printed in China by RR Donnelley
for David & Charles
Brunel House, Newton Abbot, Devon

Publisher Alison Myer
Acquisitions Editor Jennifer Fox-Proverbs
Assistant Editor Jeni Hennah
Project Editor Cheryl Brown
Senior Designer and Illustrator Mia Trenoweth
Photographer Sian Irvine
Production Controller Beverley Richardson
Pre Press Natasha Jorden

David & Charles publish high quality books on a wide range of
subjects. For more great book ideas visit: **www.rucraft.co.uk**

Contents

Introduction

I have been sewing and creating for as long as I can remember. I have wonderful early memories of my lovely mum making toys for the school fete at the dining-room table. There was always a large bowl filled with dolls' eyes and animal noses, needles and threads, buttons and lace, fur and fabric, bits of stuffing and pattern remnants. Famous for her rag dolls and their beautifully embroidered faces, she always let me have first pick of her creations before donating the rest. I loved our regular trips to the shop with the glass-fronted drawers where she would buy me a tray cloth and threads to embroider it with, and I still have those early efforts today.

I don't really remember mum teaching me to sew; it was just always part of our everyday life, and sewing seemed such a natural thing for me to do. So when I became a mother, I adorned my four beautiful children with homemade toys, hand-sewn clothes and fancy dress costumes, and brought them up in the same environment as my mother had with me. Consequently, they are all very creative and able to occupy themselves for hours with a needle, thread and a scrap of fabric. Recently my eleven-year-old son astonished me with the gorgeous blanket stitch he had sewn on a Christmas decoration he had made for his sister. When I asked him who had taught him such a neat stitch, he replied, 'No one, I just watched you'.

My aim in this book is to encourage you to pick up a needle and thread; stitch something, make something – use it, give it, love it. Discover what a really great feeling it can be. The 20 project ideas featured are all quick-and-easy to make to allow you time to focus on embroidering the wonderful designs using just 11 simple stitches. There are eight great motif chapters to get you stitching, from bunnies to buttons and cooking to Christmas. I have chosen a classic colour scheme of taupe, cream and red so that your precious 'makes' will look just as good in ten years' time as they do today. Begin by reading through Get Ready to Stitch, then pick up your needle and thread and get started. And always remember my motto:

Sew what you like, like what you sew.

Get Ready to Stitch

If you are new to stitching, this chapter will give you all the advice you need to begin with confidence. Luckily most items required for stitching can be found in an everyday sewing basket. The embroideries are hand-stitched, but a sewing machine has been used to make up the projects and I have included some best practice tips here.

I have given details of the fabrics and threads I have used with tips to help you get started with your own sewing stash. There is a guide to the different ways you can transfer embroidery motifs to your fabric, and the section on working the stitches has instructions for both right- and left-handed stitchers. So what are you waiting for? Get stitching!

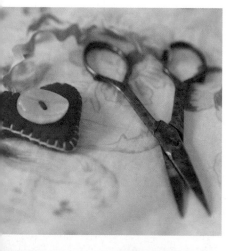

Fabrics and Braids

Just so long as it's natural and a needle slices through it like butter, I will stitch it. I have an ever-growing collection of fabrics and braids and I encourage you to start your fabric stash today. Look out for lovely linens and cottons wherever you go and buy pretty trims and buttons to ensure your stitching stands out from the rest.

Linens and cottons

I love to scour second-hand shops looking for opportunities to recycle clothing and household linens to build my fabric collection. I rummage for recycled tray cloths and linens whenever the opportunity arises. I've even been known to cut up my best linen trousers (they were too tight!). Get in the habit of visiting fabric and patchwork shops to keep an eye on their stock – buying bolt ends and off-cuts can help to boost your stash.

Felt

There is really only one felt that I would recommend you use and that is wool felt. Without the wool, felt will not last and is poor quality. At the very least, you should choose a wool/mix felt.

Wool blanket

The wool blanket I used for the Heart Blanket has 20% polyester in it making it machine washable. A recycled wool blanket would also be a perfect choice but take care when laundering to avoid shrinkage.

Preparing fabrics for stitching

It is advisable to wash and press your fabrics before you sew and this is particularly important for red fabrics in case the colour runs. Fabrics are often treated with a sort of starch dressing to make them easier to sew; so after washing and drying your fabrics, you may find that giving them a little spray starch will aid sewing.

Buttons and braids

I love to add decorative tapes and pretty buttons to embellish my hand-stitched projects. There is a lovely variety available, and I recommend you keep a good collection to inspire you. Ric-rac is a great favourite of mine – it can be sewn on by machine or by hand using backstitch or a stitch similar to herringbone. However, there are a few pitfalls, so do follow the instructions for working with ric-rac braid in the Techniques section. To attach other decorative braids, sew down each side of the tape in a thread that matches the main fabric colour. As for buttons, you will be spoilt for choice. I love to use buttons from my vintage collection, or unusual ones that I have found on my fabric shopping trips like the super little heart-shaped buttons used for the holly berries on the Christmas Tree Decorations. And there is always the option to make your own embroidered buttons (see Techniques).

I store my ribbons and tapes in a wooden box. You can wind them around a decorative form to keep them neat; alternatively, wrap around your fingers and tie or pin to prevent them from unravelling.

Needles and Threads

I am a keen recycler of fabrics, but I'd urge caution with needles and threads – old needles may develop little rust spots and thread deteriorates over time. The threads I prefer are described below but do experiment with other thicknesses and types. Stitchers fall in love with their special needle – when you find yours, keep it safe!

Coton à broder

A favourite of mine, this single strand thread has a matt finish. It is available in different widths in several colours. I prefer No.16 which is quite thick and ideal for blanket stitching, outlining, backstitching, and quilting. Shops rarely stock the whole range but they can be ordered. To keep neat and ready to use remove the paper label and unwind the skein. Cut through all the threads at the knot. Fold in half and place the loop end over a small door knob. Divide into three and plait firmly to the end (see photo, right). Pull a new thread from the looped end. The remaining threads will stay plaited while the thread removed is the perfect length for sewing.

Perle

This high-sheen single strand thread has a slight twist to it. It is available in skeins or balls in different thicknesses from No.3 (thick) to No.12 (thin), and I prefer No.8. It produces a thick stitching line with a slight texture to it and makes a good substitute for coton à broder.

Stranded cotton (floss)

This is available in skeins consisting of six strands which can be pulled out individually for use. It is most usual to use two strands in the needle, but for fine detail use just one, and for a chunkier stitching line use three or more.

Needles

Invest in a pack of good-quality mixed embroidery needles. These have large eyes and are very sharp, piercing the fabric and allowing the thread to be pulled through with very little friction. How do you know what size needle to use? If after three attempts the needle won't thread, change to one with a larger hole. *Threading a needle* To use a needle threader, push the wire loop through the needle eye; push the thread through the wire loop. Gently pull the needle threader back out of the hole and it will bring the thread with it.

Thread-wise

- Coton à broder is available in a large variety of colours that match with stranded cotton (floss) colours.
- If you prefer, you can substitute a single coton à broder or perle thread for two strands of stranded cotton (floss).
- Good-quality thread brands will be colourfast; they will not run and spoil your work. If using recycled threads of an unknown origin, always test for colourfastness before using on your embroidery.
- Be aware threads can deteriorate with age – colours fade and they may be weakened.
- As well as embroidery threads, you will also need sewing threads to make up your projects. Use a good-quality thread in a colour to match your fabric.

Transferring the Motifs

Before beginning your embroidery you need to transfer your chosen design from the Motif section onto your fabric. There are many ways to do this. Choose the method that best suits your fabric and design, and remember you must be able to see the outline clearly to embroider it, but it should not be visible on the finished project.

Iron-on transfer pencil

Use to trace the motif onto tracing paper. Place the tracing paper onto your fabric, right sides facing and iron (without steam). This transferral method is useful for fabrics that you cannot see through such as thicker linens and wools, but the motif will be reversed. The transferred line is permanent and cannot be erased so you will need to hide it with your embroidery stitches, and you must sharpen the pencil frequently to avoid a thick drawn line. As this pencil is only available in red, it will not work on the darker red fabrics used for some of the projects in this book.

Pencil

This is my preferred method for tracing the design when I can see through the fabric. If you use either pencils sharpened to a point or good quality propelling pencils, the mark will be so fine that it will not require erasing. There is a propelling pencil available that has changeable coloured leads, which is a good option for darker fabrics.

Water colour pencil

This is another great option for working on different coloured fabrics as the pencils are available in a variety of colours; be sure to keep the leads well sharpened to maintain a fine line. The marks will wash out when rubbed with a damp cotton bud.

Dressmaker's pencil

These are readily available in most fabric shops, and come in pink, blue and white for marking both light and dark fabrics. It is not possible to get a fine point on the pencil, but as the marked line can be brushed off or washed out, this is not such a problem.

Pens

Fade away pens Beware as marks made with these may fade before you have finished stitching. Do not iron the marked lines or expose them to heat as they may become permanent or leave an unsightly stain.

Washable pens Lines marked with these pens will wash out or can be erased with a damp cotton bud but test on your fabric first. I once had a nasty experience where years later a yellow stain could be seen on my embroidery where the marked line had been.

Permanent pen It is very important for you to be able to see the marked lines clearly. This pen's fine tip makes a clear strong line especially on smaller projects. It is, however, very permanent.

Dressmaker's carbon paper

This is available in white, blue, pink and yellow, so should mark all fabric colours. Place the paper on the fabric, right sides together. Place the tracing or template on top and draw around the design with a ball point pen. Work on a hard flat surface and press very firmly (it may be a good idea to tape down the fabric so that it doesn't move). The transferred line can sometimes be quite thick and it doesn't always come out successfully.

A fade away pen works well on light fabrics.

White dressmaker's carbon paper stands out clearly on darker fabrics.

Card template

A card template is a good method to choose when your fabric is too dark to see through or you have an easy repeat shape to transfer. I used it for the hearts on the Heart Blanket and the seed packets on the Gardener's Tidy. Trace the motif onto paper, stick it onto lightweight card and carefully cut out. Place the template on the fabric as required and trace around the outside with a fine pencil.

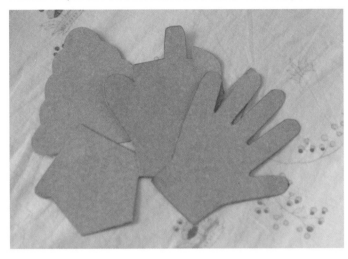

As an alternative to a light box tape the design to the window, tape your fabric on top and trace off.

Light box

A great aid for tracing motifs onto lighter fabrics, a light box is both reasonably priced and readily available; alternatively, you can make one from a strong plastic or heavy cardboard box. Fix a light fitting inside and clip a piece of perspex on top.

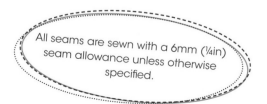

All seams are sewn with a 6mm (¼in) seam allowance unless otherwise specified.

Making the Projects

I have designed over 20 easy-to-make projects for you to embellish with stitching. For more detailed instructions on using a sewing machine, working with fusible webbing, edging with ric-rac braid, custom-made bias binding, and making covered buttons, refer to the Techniques section at the end of the book.

Sewing by hand or machine

I have used a sewing machine to make all of the projects in this book, although they can be made entirely by hand if you so choose. But if you have access to a sewing machine, do use it. It is so much faster, leaving more time for the stitching which is the fun bit. Some helpful tips on using a sewing machine are included in the Techniques section. Whether you choose to stitch your chosen projects by hand or machine, there are a couple of hand finishing stitches you will need.

Ladder stitch

For closing a seam on a stuffed item or sewing two folded edges together. The stitches look like a ladder until they are pulled tight to close the seam. Knot the end of the thread and start from inside the opening to hide the knot. Take straight stitches into the folded fabric, stitching into each edge in turn. After a few stitches pull the thread taut to draw up the stitches and close the gap.

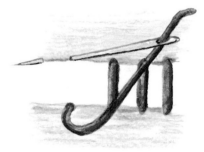

Slip stitch

Also used to close gaps in seams. When worked neatly, it is almost invisible. Work from right to left, picking up a tiny piece of the fabric from one seam edge. Insert the needle into the other seam fold and move the needle along 3mm (⅛in). Push the needle out into the seam edge and repeat.

Working the Stitches

I have selected 11 simple decorative hand stitches for my designs. If you have not embroidered since your school days, take the time to refresh your memory of how these are worked. The stitches required for each project are listed alongside the 'you will need' listing. Practise them first on a linen scrap following the instructions for right- or left-handed stitchers as appropriate.

Using an embroidery hoop

It is a matter of personal preference as to whether or not you use an embroidery hoop to keep your fabric taut while stitching. I prefer not to as I find it gets in my way and yet I still produce lovely work with no lumps or bumps. Embroidery hoops come in two parts, a smaller hoop and a slightly larger one with a tension screw on one side. They can be made of wood or plastic, although plastic ones may not have a tension screw. Place the fabric you are going to embroider over the smaller hoop. Place the larger hoop over the fabric and push it onto the smaller hoop – you will find that the larger hoop is stretchy to enable you to do this. Pull the fabric taut and tighten the tension screw. The fabric is now ready to embroider.

Starting and finishing stitching

♥ Iron-on lightweight interfacing can be ironed over the back of the work to hide the knots and stray ends.

♥ Thread your needle – never use more than a short arm's length of thread at one time as it will be more prone to knotting, and more vulnerable to fraying and splitting.

♥ Start the embroideries with a small knot on the wrong side of the work. To avoid the knot being seen from the front of the work, do keep it small.

♥ When rejoining a thread, use your needle to weave the new thread into the previous stitches.

♥ When you have finished your embroidery, weave the thread into the previous sewn work.

♥ Do not leave long strands hanging on the back as these may show through on the front.

Keep your embroidery and fabric scissors sharp and never be tempted to use them for cutting paper.

You may find a hoop useful when stitching the infill chain stitching.

RUNNING STITCH

Run the needle in and out of the fabric for a simple but versatile line stitch.

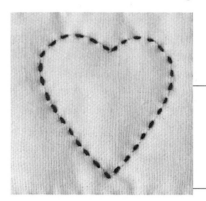

Can be used to:

❀ Outline and accentuate shapes

❀ Create veins in leaves

❀ Sew two layers together

You can take more than one stitch on your needle at a time, but take care to keep stitches even.

No one said running stitch had to run in a straight line. In this detail from the Gardener's Tidy it is used to indicate the buzzing bee's flight path, and it has the added advantage of sewing the back and front layers of fabric together.

Right-handers

Work from right to left. Bring the needle up through the fabric, make a stitch, and bring the needle down through the fabric again. Repeat, making sure the stitches and the spaces between the stitches are the same size.

start

Left-handers

Work from left to right. Bring the needle up through the fabric, make a stitch, and bring the needle down through the fabric again. Repeat, making sure the stitches and the spaces between the stitches are the same size.

start

BACKSTITCH
This is the perfect stitch when a well-defined outline is required.

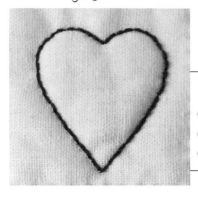

Can be used to:

❀ Outline shapes and highlight details

❀ Write words and numbers

❀ Create flower stems

Right-handers

Work from right to left. Begin by bringing the needle up a little ahead of where you want the line of stitching to start. Take the needle to the right, to the start position, back through the fabric to make a stitch, and bring it out to the left past the first stitch.

Left-handers

Work from left to right. Begin by bringing the needle up a little ahead of where you want to start the stitching. Take the needle to the left, to the start position, back through the fabric to make a stitch, and bring it out to the right past the first stitch.

Although this needs a little practise to get neat and even, an uneven stitch can look nice too.

Each time a stitch is made, the thread passes back to fill the gap, for small stitches of an equal length.

Each time a stitch is made, the thread passes back to fill the gap, for small stitches of an equal length.

STEM STITCH

An outline stitch with neatly overlapping lines.

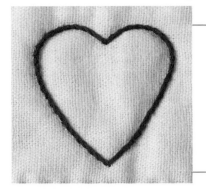

Can be used to:

❀ Represent the stems of flowers as detail, right

❀ Follow curves easily, but not on small motifs

❀ Create texture

Right-handers

Work from left to right. Bring the needle up at the start point and make a stitch forward. Take a tiny stitch backwards from right to left. Pull the needle through, keeping the thread above the needle.

Keep your stitches quite small as they do tend to grow in length.

Take another small stitch to the right bringing the needle out near the hole of the last stitch.

As you continue to stitch the stitches take on a diagonal slant.

Left-handers

Work from right to left. Bring the needle up at the start point and make a stitch backward. Take a tiny stitch forwards from left to right. Pull the needle through, keeping the thread above the needle.

Take another small stitch to the left bringing the needle out near the hole of the last stitch.

As you continue to stitch the stitches take on a diagonal slant.

CHAIN STITCH
A series of looped stitches worked to form a chain-like pattern.

Aim for an even row of equally spaced stitches.

Can be used to:
- ❀ Outline an embroidery motif
- ❀ Create flower stems
- ❀ Fill in a shape when worked in close rows as detail, right

Right-handers

Work from right to left. Bring the needle and thread up at the start point. Holding the thread to the left, put the needle back in where it first came out and bring the needle tip out again a little way beyond this point. Make sure the thread is under the needle and gently pull through.

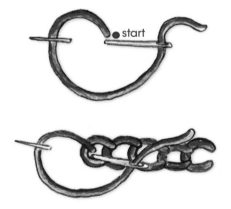

Put the needle in again beside the last stitch and continue. To secure the final stitch, sew a small straight stitch over the final loop.

Left-handers

Work from left to right. Bring the needle and thread up at the start point. Holding the thread to the right, put the needle back in where it first came out and bring the needle tip out again a little way beyond this point. Make sure the thread is under the needle and gently pull through.

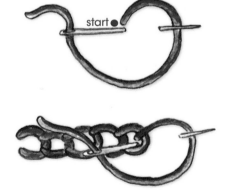

Put the needle in again beside the last stitch and continue. To secure the final stitch, sew a small straight stitch over the final loop.

LAZY DAISY
A very pretty stitch related to the chain stitch.

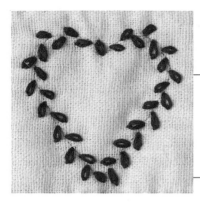

Can be used to:
- ❀ Make lovely flowers
- ❀ Create perfect leaves
- ❀ Embroider seeds when worked very small

Right-handers

Work from left to right. Bring the needle up through the fabric at the top of the petal, hold the thread down with your thumb. Reinsert the needle at the start point and take it up again at the petal tip, keeping the thread under the needle.

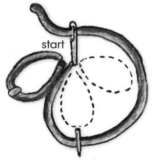

start

Pull the thread through and, holding the petal down, make a little stitch at the tip to secure.

Left-handers

Work from right to left. Bring the needle up through the fabric at the top of the petal, hold the thread down with your thumb. Reinsert the needle at the start point and take it up again at the petal tip, keeping the thread under the needle.

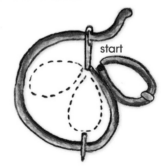

start

Pull the thread through and, holding the petal down, make a little stitch at the tip to secure.

If you pull the stitches tight you get long thin petals, if you sew them loosely they are plump and fat.

WHIPPED RUNNING STITCH
Whip a second thread through a line of running stitch for a decorative variation on this simple stitch.

Can be used to:
❀ Outline curved motifs
❀ Create a textured braided effect
❀ Decorate with contrasting threads

To prevent piercing through either the thread or the fabric, use the eye of the needle to whip the thread over the running stitches.

Right-handers
Start by sewing the motif with a running stitch. For the best effect, keep the running stitches small. Working from right to left, pull the thread up from behind at the start point and slip the needle over and under one of the running stitches. Continue to whip the thread over in this way until all the running stitches are covered.

start

Left-handers
Start by sewing the motif with a running stitch. For the best effect, keep the running stitches small. Working from left to right, pull the thread up from behind at the start point and slip the needle over and under one of the running stitches. Continue to whip the thread over in this way until all the running stitches are covered.

start

Working the second thread with a contrasting thread colour creates a wonderful braided effect, which is just perfect for the jam jar lid string in this detail from the Shelf Bunting.

BLANKET STITCH
This is a great border or edging stitch.

Aim to keep the tops of the stitches level.

Can be used to:
❀ Appliqué fabric shapes onto a background fabric

❀ Outline seed packet labels

❀ Define the edge of self-covered buttons

Right-handers

Work from left to right. Bring the needle up on the line of the motif or the edge of the appliqué. Take a stitch down from the line and bring the needle back where you started keeping the thread to the left.

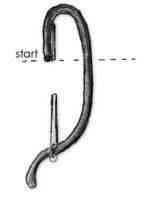

start

Insert the needle to the right of the first stitch, down from the line or edge, and bring it back out on the line or edge, making sure the thread is behind the needle. Pull through.

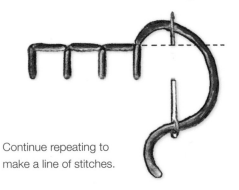

Continue repeating to make a line of stitches.

Left-handers

Work from right to left. Bring the needle up on the line of the motif or the edge of the appliqué. Take a stitch down from and bring the needle back where you started keeping the thread to the right

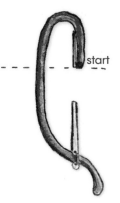

start

Insert the needle to the left of the first stitch, down from the line or edge, and bring it back out on the line or edge, making sure the thread is behind the needle. Pull through.

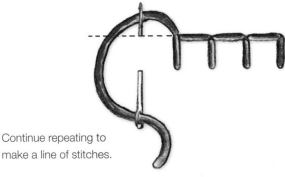

Continue repeating to make a line of stitches.

HERRINGBONE STITCH
A little tricky to get right, but well worth it as this stitch looks great even in small doses.

Can be used to:

❀ Outline a border

❀ Decorate a plain braid

❀ Add decorative interest to a hem

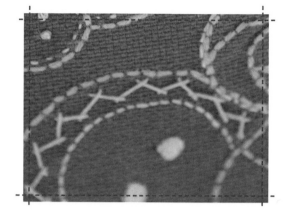

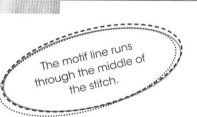

The motif line runs through the middle of the stitch.

I love the look of this stitch but mine seem to get bigger as I go along. It is worth persisting as the results can look fantastic.

Right-handers

Work from left to right. Bring the needle up below the motif line, cross over to the top right and take a little stitch to the left above the line.

start

Cross over to the bottom right, and take a little stitch to the left. The needle should come out directly below the stitch above. Continue to line up the top end of a diagonal stitch with the bottom start of another for a nice, even line of stitching.

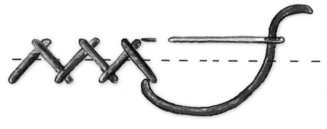

Left-handers

Work from right to left. Bring the needle up below the motif line, cross over to the top left and take a little stitch to the right above the line.

start

Cross over to the bottom left, and take a little stitch to the right. The needle should come out directly below the stitch above. Continue to line up the top end of a diagonal stitch with the bottom start of another for a nice, even line of stitching.

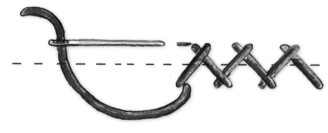

FRENCH KNOT
A useful and cute stitch that must be mastered.

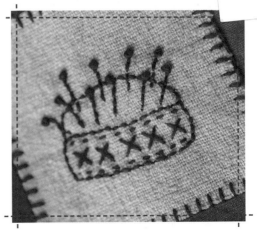

For a larger or smaller knot wrap the thread around the needle more or less times.

Can be used to:
❀ Add eyes
❀ Form a flower centre
❀ Give decorative detail and texture

Right-handers

Bring the needle up from the back of the fabric, and wrap the thread around the needle two or three times. Put the needle back into the fabric close to where it originally came out. *Do not* go back into the same hole otherwise the knot will be lost.

Left-handers

Bring the needle up from the back of the fabric, and wrap the thread around the needle two or three times. Put the needle back into the fabric close to where it originally came out. *Do not* go back into the same hole otherwise the knot will be lost.

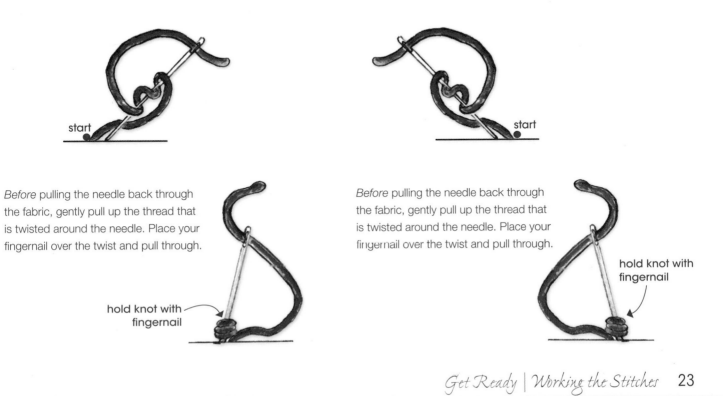

start

start

Before pulling the needle back through the fabric, gently pull up the thread that is twisted around the needle. Place your fingernail over the twist and pull through.

Before pulling the needle back through the fabric, gently pull up the thread that is twisted around the needle. Place your fingernail over the twist and pull through.

hold knot with fingernail

hold knot with fingernail

CROSS STITCH

Most often seen worked in groups, discover the decorative power of the individual cross stitch.

Can be used to:

✿ Decorate with 'one off' stitches

✿ Create a star stitch when worked one on top of the other as detail, right

✿ Pretty up a plain ribbon

Right-handers

Work from left to right. Bring the needle up through the fabric. Take a stitch diagonally from the top left to the bottom right and bring the needle back out at the lower left corner.

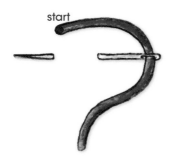

Take a stitch diagonally to the top right corner and bring the needle back where the next cross stitch is required. Pull the needle through to complete the cross stitch.

Left-handers

Work from right to left. Bring the needle up through the fabric. Take a stitch diagonally from the top right to the bottom left and bring the needle back out at the lower right corner.

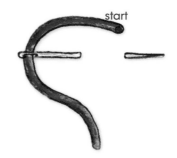

Take a stitch diagonally to the top left corner and bring the needle back out where the next cross stitch is required. Pull the needle through to complete the cross stitch.

SATIN STITCH
A filling stitch used to create a smooth surface decoration – a little bit painful but occasionally necessary.

Can be used to:
❀ Fill small shapes
❀ Make lovely small hearts
❀ Embroider buttonholes

For best results use sharp needles and finer threads like stranded cottons (floss).

Right-handers

Work from right to left. Start on one side of the motif and take the stitches across from side to side, keeping them very even and close to each other. Try to avoid stacking the stitches on top of each other or the effect will be unattractively lumpy. The stitches can be worked in a slanting direction or straight across the design.

Left-handers

Work from left to right. Start on one side of the motif and take the stitches across from side to side, keeping them very even and close to each other. Try to avoid stacking the stitches on top of each other or the effect will be unattractively lumpy. The stitches can be worked in a slanting direction or straight across the design.

start

start

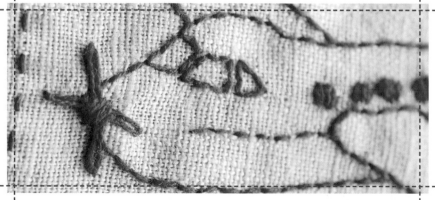

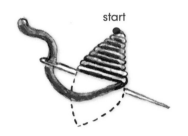

The centre of the plane's propeller on the Luggage Tag is worked with satin stitch.

Hearts

The heart motif has a timeless appeal, so I make no excuses for using it on many of the projects in this book. Heart-shaped buttons adorn the pockets of the Sew Tidy hanging in the Sewing chapter, stitched hearts decorate the Baby's Record Book in the Baby Bunny chapter, and felt hearts garland the Christmas tree in the Christmas chapter. It is the perfect design to use when you are making gifts for those you love, and it is an easy shape to practise your stitches on as it has gentle curves and straight lines. You could stitch your own heart sampler using nine of the stitch details from Working the Stitches arranged in a simple nine-square grid, or for a first-time project with great impact, get started on the Heart Blanket.

Heart Blanket

There is nothing nicer than wrapping yourself up in a cosy blanket on a chilly evening. This generous coverlet is such a simple project to make, and its easy-to-embroider heart motif samples nine of the stitches found in the book. I have used wool blanketing which was lovely to stitch on, but fleece is easier to find and works just as well.

The blanket's big but beautiful hearts are quick to stitch using a chunky yarn. If you want to practise the same stitches using embroidery threads, the Heart Cushion gives you the chance with its delightful stacked heart design.

If you prefer you can use a good quality fleece in place of the wool blanket, but you will need to make sure that you use a very sharp darning needle for embroidering the hearts. Both blanket and fleece can be difficult to mark. Try dressmaker's pencil or washable pen but do test first on a piece of scrap fabric.

You will need

- ♡ 122cm x 122cm (48in x 48in) wool blanket
- ♡ 8m (8½yd) narrow ric-rac
- ♡ 5m (5½yd) of 4cm (1½in) wide binding tape
- ♡ 50g (1¾oz) double knit (worsted) cotton or wool yarn
- ♡ Coton à broder: red, two skeins
- ♡ Large darning needle

note: binding tape can be bought ready-to-use in a variety of colours and a few limited pattern ranges or you can make your own (see Techniques).

Finished size: 122cm x 122cm (48in x 48in)

Preparing the blanket

1. Divide the blanket into sixteen 30.5cm (12in) squares and tack the divisions with a large running stitch.

2. Make a card template of the largest heart motif (see Heart Motifs). Use the template to mark a heart in the centre of each of the squares, lining up the hearts vertically and horizontally. I have chosen to place the final heart (top left-hand corner) at an angle. This is a good place to sew your initials, name, or a little message. Use the alphabet (see Alphabet Motifs) to transfer the letters of your choice.

3. Cut the ric-rac into six 127cm (50in) lengths and pin onto the tacked division lines. Using the coton à broder in an ordinary sewing needle, sew the ric-rac in place by hand following Fig. 1.

Fig. 1

Stitches used

Chain stitch
Running stitch
Whipped running stitch
Herringbone stitch
French knot
Blanket stitch
Cross stitch
Stem stitch
Lazy daisy

note: For transferring the embroidery design, use card templates (see Transferring the Motifs).

4. Using the yarn threaded in the darning needle, embroider the hearts following the stitch key (Fig. 2).

Fig. 2

chain	running	whipped	herringbone
herringbone	french knot	blanket	running
whipped	cross stitch	stem	chain
running	lazy daisy	herringbone	blanket

Key to stitches.

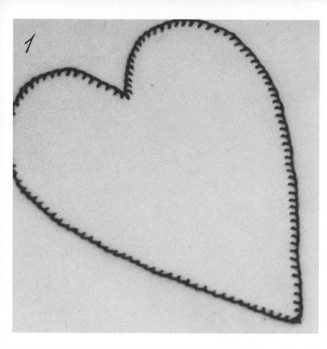

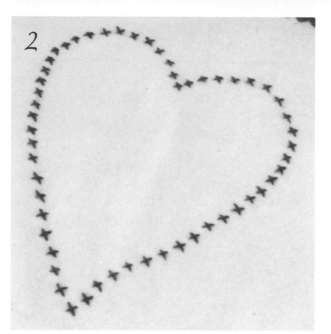

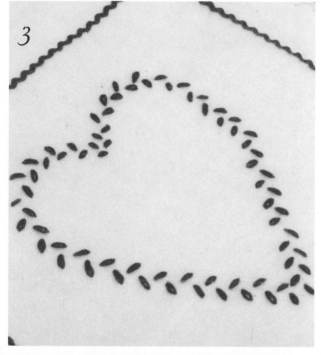

Embroidering the hearts

❀ Stitch each heart following the stitch key (Fig. 2). Do make sure that you are very neat when starting and finishing off each heart as the stitching will be seen on the back. Rather than using a knot to begin, leave a long length of yarn at the start of your stitching and weave in once the embroidery is complete.

❀ All of the stitches except the lazy daisy are worked following the marked heart line as the blanket stitch (1) and cross stitch (2) details shown. Start stitching in the V-shape at the top of the heart.

❀ The lazy daises are worked along either side of the marked heart (3). Begin your first stitch on the outside of the marked line and sew it at a 45-degree angle to the line. Now bring the needle back up on the inside of the line directly opposite the end of the first stitch, and stitch another lazy daisy. Continue alternating the stitches in this way all the way around the heart.

❀ Finish by adding your initials, name or message to the top left hand heart. I have used a backstitch, but a stem or running stitch would work just as well.

Binding the blanket

1. Working with the right side of the blanket facing you, lay the binding tape half way down along one side, matching the raw edges. Pin in place. (Only pin the binding to the side you are working on; when you have completed the mitre of the first corner, you can then pin the next side, and so on.) Starting 15.5cm (6in) from the beginning of the binding, machine sew using a generous 6mm (¼in) seam. If you are using ready-made bias binding you will have to open out one folded edge to pin it to the blanket edge.

2. Stitch until you reach one corner, stopping *exactly* 6mm (¼in) from the end (Fig. 3).

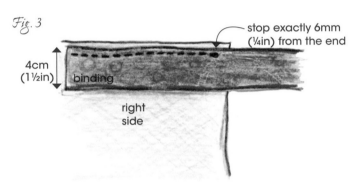

Fig. 3

stop exactly 6mm (¼in) from the end

4cm (1½in)

binding

right side

3. Pull the work away from the machine. Fold the binding up so that it is aligned with the edge of the blanket as shown in Fig. 4, making sure that it is straight.

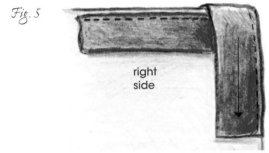

Fig. 4

fold

right side

4. Holding the corner, fold the binding back down, aligning it with the raw edge and making sure that the folded corner is square. Pin and sew over the fold continuing down the next side (Fig. 5).

Fig. 5

right side

5. Continue to bind around the remaining sides following Figs. 3–5 at each corner. Stop stitching 15.5cm (6in) from the end. Lay both ends of the binding along the blanket's edge and fold them back where they meet. Finger press the folds well. Trim to 6mm (¼in) from the folded ends, and stitch together (Fig. 6). Open out and finger press the seam. Complete the sewing of the binding along the edge.

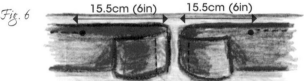

Fig. 6

15.5cm (6in)   15.5cm (6in)

trim the folded ends to 6mm (¼in) and seam together

6. Once all four edges have been sewn, fold the binding over to the wrong side and slip stitch in place. The corners mitre beautifully on their own, all you need to do is slip stitch them closed (Fig. 7).

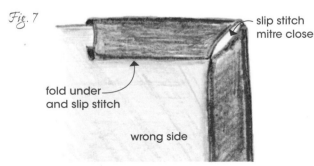

Fig. 7

slip stitch mitre close

fold under and slip stitch

wrong side

Heart Cushion

Hearts are such an endearing shape that I couldn't resist making a second project. The heart cushion is made exactly as the Nursery Cushion in the Baby Bunny chapter. Transfer the stacked heart design (see Heart Motifs) onto the cushion top using dressmaker's carbon paper. Back with wadding and embroider the design using two skeins of taupe coton à broder and following the stitch key marked on the design. Note, the herringbone stitch border is worked following the outline of the chain stitch as a guide. Fasten the envelope back with a large embroidered felt button made in the same way as the buttons on the Button Bracelet in the Buttons chapter.

Sewing

Now that you've discovered the joys of stitching, you'll love the Sewing Motifs that celebrate your new passion. Buttons and threads, pincushions and scissors, all your most important sewing kit is pictured here. I believe that you need to have the right tools for the job, but they can be gorgeous looking too. So I have designed the Time to Sew stitching set especially for you. This needle roll, pincushion and tape measure trio are your essential basics, but why stop there? Make a Sew Tidy and fill it with your fabrics, patterns, scissors, pens and pencils. Or make a Little Sew Bag, a smaller version of the Button Bag seen in the Buttons chapter, for stitching to go.

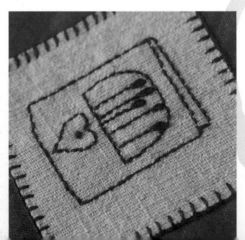

Time to Sew

This must-have set provides new stitchers with their three sewing essentials. The wristwatch-style pincushion wraps around the wrist ready for action, pinning hems and fixing curtains. But you won't get far without a tape measure, so I have created a clever little cover to match the pincushion wristwatch.

Complete your set with the easy-to-make needle roll with its stitched compartments for storing different-sized needles. The rolled case is fastened off with a lovely sewing themed button.

Make time to sew with this essential collection of needlework basics. The pincushion fits neatly round your wrist, and the second clock face disguises a retractable tape measure cover. Just pull the winder button to reveal the tape, and once you have finished measuring, retract by pressing the cute little heart button on the back.

Pin Cushion

You will need

- Two 7.5cm (3in) squares linen
- 19cm x 4cm (7½in x 1½in) linen strip
- Sewing thread to match
- 7.5cm (3in) square thin cotton wadding
- Stranded cotton (floss): red and taupe, one skein each
- Red buttons, two medium and one small heart-shaped
- 19cm x 2cm (7½in x ¾in) heavy interfacing
- Thin card
- Template plastic
- 22cm x 3.2cm (8½in x 1¼in) red wool felt
- 20cm x 1.3cm (8in x ½in) decorative tape
- Handful of stuffing
- One large red popper

Finished size: 5.5cm (2³⁄₁₆in) watch face diameter

Making the watch face

1. Take one of the 7.5cm (3in) linen squares and, using the carbon paper method, transfer the watch face motif onto it (see Sewing Motifs).

2. Place the wadding on the back of the fabric behind the transferred design. Tack in place. Note, you will be embroidering through both layers to create a quilted effect, and the circle shape is cut after the embroidery is completed.

3. Embroider the design (see Embroidering the watch face, opposite). Once the embroidery is complete, and working from behind, cut away the wadding very close to the blanket stitch.

4. Cut the embroidered linen square into a rough circle. With double thread, sew a row of gathering stitches around the outside of the circle. Use the watch face motif to cut out a circle from the thin card. Place the cardboard circle in the middle of the back of the fabric circle and pull up the gathering stitches.

Stitches used

Blanket stitch
Backstitch
Satin stitch
French knot
Herringbone stitch

You can recycle flat plastic from an old document folder just so long as it is thick enough that a pin will not go through it.

5. Take the linen strip and embroider a row of herringbone stitches along the middle of it.

6. Tack the strip of heavy interfacing to the back of the embroidered linen strip. Position the interfacing so that it is central with a 6mm (¼in) seam free at each short end. Fold in half right sides together and sew a 6mm (¼in) seam; open out the seam. You now have a continuous fabric circle. Turn the fabric over the interfacing and tack in place. Turn the right way out.

7. Pin the sides of the watch to the watch face so that the sewn seam at the side is at 3 o'clock. Sew the two together using double thread and a ladder stitch.

8. Sew one of the medium buttons over the side seam to represent the watch winder. Gently remove the card circle from the watch face. Put to one side.

9. Cut the remaining square of linen into a rough circle and, using double thread, sew a row of gathering stitches around the outside edge. Use the cardboard circle to cut out a circle from template plastic. Gather the linen around the plastic and fasten off securely. Put to one side.

Embroidering the watch face

❀ Use two strands of the red embroidery thread in your needle.
❀ Blanket stitch around the outline of the watch face making a longer stitch on the five-minute markers.
❀ Backstitch the numbers and the hands of the watch.
❀ Satin stitch the two hearts at the end of the hands.
❀ Sew on a small heart button in the middle of the watch face.
❀ Add French knots to the ends of the five-minute markers.

Assembling the watch

1. Take the wool felt strip and sew the length of decorative tape in the middle of it. Blanket stitch each side and both ends of the felt strip using two strands of the taupe stranded cotton (floss).

2. Pin the watch back to the wrong side of the strap (Fig. 1). Sew to join keeping your stitches neat and discreet.

3. Lay the strap on your work surface so that it is running from top to bottom with the right side of the strap facing. Place the watch face over the watch back so that 12 o'clock is at the top (see Fig. 1); pin. Ladder stitch together leaving a small gap for the stuffing. Stuff firmly and sew the opening closed.

4. Sew the two halves of the popper, one on the back at the top of the strap and the other at the front of the bottom of the strap. To finish, sew the remaining button at the front of the top of the strap for a false button effect.

Fig. 1

sew popper to front

stitch to base

stitch to base

wrong side of watch back

leave open

right side of watch strap

sew popper to back

You can sew a row of chain stitch around the top and bottom of the watch face to define its edges and hide untidy seams.

Tape Measure

You will need

- ♥ Two 7.5cm (3in) squares linen
- ♥ 18cm x 2.5cm (7in x 1in) linen strip
- ♥ 18cm x 6mm (7in x ¼in) narrow decorative tape
- ♥ Thin card
- ♥ 16.5cm x 1.3cm (6½in x ½in) heavy interfacing
- ♥ 7.5cm (3in) square thin cotton wadding
- ♥ Stranded cotton (floss): red, one skein
- ♥ Red buttons, one medium and two small heart-shaped
- ♥ 5.7cm (2¼in) retractable tape measure

Finished size: 5.7cm (2¼in) watch face diameter

Making the tape measure cover

1. Follow steps 1–4 of the pincushion. Sew the narrow decorative tape down the middle of the linen strip, machining along each side.

2. Turn the strip over and tack the heavy interfacing to its back making sure that it is centred. Turn the excess fabric over the interfacing on all four sides and tack in place. Blanket stitch the two short ends to complete the tape measure cover side.

3. Leaving the card template in place, pin the side to the top leaving a 6mm (¼in) gap at 3 o'clock. This will be the opening for the tape measure tag to be pulled out from.

4. To make the base, cut the remaining linen square into a rough circle and sew a row of gathering stitches around the outside edge with double thread. Gather the linen around a cardboard circle and fasten off securely. Replace the cardboard circle with a circle of wadding.

5. Put the tape measure inside the watch matching the tape tag with the opening on the side; pin on the base and ladder stitch in place. Sew a medium button onto the end of the tape measure tag, and a heart button on the back to indicate the position of the tape measure's retracting button.

Stitches used (tape measure)

Blanket stitch
Backstitch
Satin stitch
French knot

Stitches used (needle roll)

Blanket stitch
French knot
Lazy daisy
Herringbone stitch
Cross stitch
Blanket stitch

note: dressmaker's carbon paper is the best way to transfer the motifs.

Needle Roll

You will need

- ♥ 9cm x 24cm (3½in x 9½in) linen for lining
- ♥ 7.5cm x 23cm (3in x 9in) felt
- ♥ Decorative tapes, two 1.3cm x 24cm (½in x 9½in), one 6mm x 25.5cm (¼in x 10in)
- ♥ 7.5cm (3in) square linen to cover button
- ♥ Lightweight interfacing
- ♥ 38mm self-cover button
- ♥ One small heart button
- ♥ Stranded cotton (floss): red and taupe, one skein each

Finished size: 7.5cm x 23.3cm (2⅞in x 9⅛in)

Making the needle roll

1. Transfer the motifs for the lining of the needle roll onto the linen strip using the dressmaker's carbon paper method (see Transferring the Motifs).

2. Embroider the design (see Embroidering the inside of the needle roll, right).

3. Press under 6mm (¼in) all the way around the outside edge of the lining.

4. Pin the 1.3cm (½in) wide tapes in place on the right side of the felt 1.3cm (½in) in from the long edges; fold the tape ends over to the wrong side of the felt. Sew down both sides of the tapes. If you wish, you can decorate the tapes with cross stitches.

5. Place the lining and felt wrong sides together and blanket stitch all the way around the outside edge using two strands of the taupe stranded cotton (floss).

Making the button and finishing off

1. Transfer the sewing button motif (see Sewing Motifs) onto the linen square. Iron on a piece of lightweight interfacing to the back of the fabric to stabilise it. Embroider the design (see Embroidering the button, right).

2. Use the embroidered linen square to make a covered button (see Techniques). Sew a row of blanket stitch around the outside edge of the button to create a nice finish.

3. Fold the needle case up towards the herringbone panel at the top. Tuck under one end of the thin tape and sew it to the right side 2.5cm (1in) in from the end of the needle roll. Sew the embroidered button on top of the tape.

4. To close the needle roll, wrap the tape around the roll and then around the button.

Use the same fabric as the lining to make the button that fastens the needle roll.

Embroidering the inside of the needle roll

❀ Use two strands of the red embroidery thread in your needle.

❀ Backstitch the outline of the design and sew a row of herringbone stitch to divide the top section. Backstitch your name in the top section and sew on a heart button to decorate.

❀ Add the detailing of the lazy daisy flower on the thimble, the French knot in the centre of the heart, and the cross stitch to the centre of the button.

Embroidering the button

❀ Using two strands of the red embroidery thread in your needle, backstitch the design and use French knots for the detailing.

Little Sew Bag

The Little Sew Bag is so useful for keeping all your sewing threads in. It is made using the same method as the Button Bag in the Buttons chapter with just a few alterations. The front of the bag has been decorated with an embroidered patch (see Sewing Motifs) worked with two strands of stranded cotton (floss) in backstitch with French knot, cross stitch and lazy daisy detailing. The patch has been blanket stitched onto the bag, and the top edge of the bag has been decorated with ric-rac. Threading the handle first through the front fastening loop, then through the back loop closes the bag.

Sew Tidy

The Sew Tidy has lots of roomy pockets to keep all your sewing bits and bobs in one place. It is made following the instructions for the Gardener's Tidy in the Garden chapter, and the middle and bottom pockets have been decorated with sewing motifs embroidered onto 5cm (2½in) linen squares that are then blanket stitched in place. To make more pockets to hold smaller things like pens, pencils, needles, I have replaced the top gusseted pocket with a straight one. To do this, cut a strip of fabric 45cm x 14cm (17½in x 5½in). Hem the top and sides and sew a piece of decorative tape along the top edge; sew in place on the tidy base. Divide into six different sized pockets giving you a variety of options for storing tools. Sew a piece of tape along the bottom edge to cover the raw edges and decorate the pockets with wooden buttons. The top of the tidy is decorated with a large felt heart sewn on with blanket stitch (see Templates). A large embroidered covered button has been sewn in the centre of the heart (see Sewing Motifs).

Cooking

We spend such a lot of time in our kitchens preparing food so, whether we love it or hate it, we should make the experience as good as possible by surrounding ourselves with lovely hand-stitched things. From fondant cream cupcakes to fruity conserves, the Cooking Motifs have inspired me to create a collection of gorgeous gifts for foodies. First on the list is a stylish apron cleverly made from a tea towel. Second, lovely bunting embroidered with jars of jam and honey and tasty teatime treats will help to brighten up kitchen shelves. And finally, an embroidered cover transforms an ordinary notebook into a treasured book of family recipes.

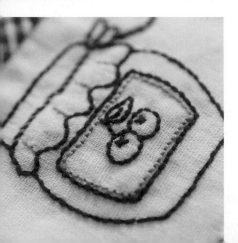

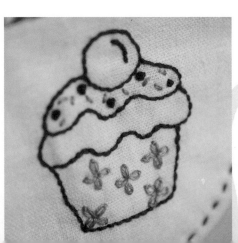

Cook's Apron

This chic apron is made from a tea towel – albeit a very nice one! I have chosen a classic striped tea towel made from a good quality, hard-working, long-lasting cotton fabric. Tea towels just like this one are so easy to find in supermarkets, department stores and even the corner shop.

When choosing a tea towel, make sure you select a woven rather than a printed one – the tea towel is folded over to create the roomy pockets, so the back of the fabric needs to look exactly the same as the front.

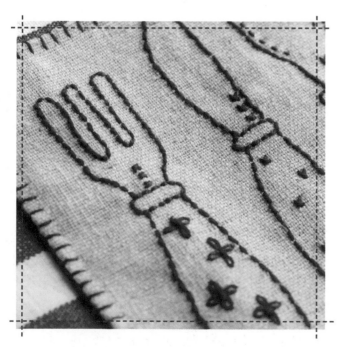

This stylish apron is the perfect gift for passionate cooks. The two pockets are spacey enough to keep the chef's essential utensils close to hand, and each has been decorated with an embroidered patch. If you want to personalise this present, you can use the alphabet in the Motifs section to add cook's initials in the centre of the plate.

You will need

- One woven tea towel, any size.
- 15.5cm x 30.5cm (6in x 12in) coordinating fabric for pocket embroidery
- Coton à broder: red, one skein
- 1m (1¼yd) wide ric-rac
- 1m (1¼yd) 5cm (2in) wide tape

Finished size: as big as your chosen tea towel

Making the apron

1. Cut the embroidery fabric in half. Using carbon paper, transfer the plate motif onto one piece and the cutlery set motif onto the other (see Cooking Motifs). Embroider the pocket patches (see opposite). Press under a 6mm (¼in) hem all the way around and tack.

2. Lay the tea towel down horizontally. To make the pockets, fold up the bottom 20cm (8in) wrong sides together. (The wrong side is the side that has been hemmed.) Press and mark the centre of the pocket area with a line of pins.

3. Sew the ric-rac along the top edge of the pocket on the right side.

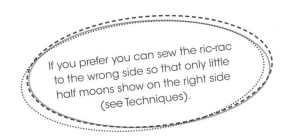

If you prefer you can sew the ric-rac to the wrong side so that only little half moons show on the right side (see Techniques).

4. Pin the embroidered panels 4cm (1½in) down from the ric-rac and 7.5cm (3in) in from either side of the pinned centre line. Blanket stitch in place.

Stitches used

Backstitch
Lazy daisy
Cross stitch
French knot
Running stitch

To coordinate your apron with your kitchen linens, buy a pack of two tea towels if you get the chance.

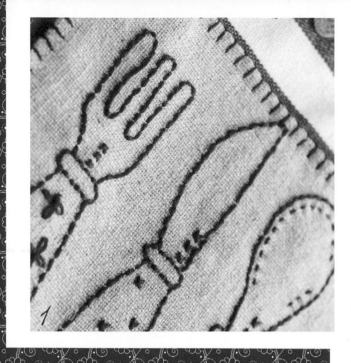

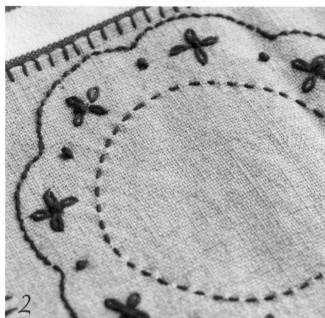

Embroidering the pocket patches

❀ Sew the outline of the cutlery set and the plate with backstitch.

❀ Decorate the handle of the fork, knife and spoon with lazy daisy, cross stitch and French knots. Add cross stitch highlights to each utensil and a line of running stitch to indicate the shape of the spoon (1).

❀ To complete the plate, embroider the inner circle with running stitch and decorate the edge with lazy daisy flowers and French knots (2).

5. Refold so that the right sides are now together. Pin both side seams close to the hem and machine stitch. Turn the right way out and press.

6. To create the two pockets, sew a double seam down the middle of the pocket area. Starting at the top of the pocket area, stitch down one side of the pins, 6mm (¼in) across the bottom, back up the other side, and 6mm (¼in) along the top. Remove the pins.

7. To make the apron ties, centre the tape along the top of the apron lining up with the edge. (To neaten the ends, before sewing in place, fold the tape over diagonally right sides together and sew a small seam along the outside edge; turn the right way out.) Sew the top, bottom and sides of the tape to the apron.

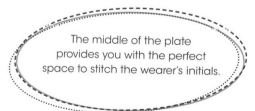

The middle of the plate provides you with the perfect space to stitch the wearer's initials.

Shelf Bunting

Bunting is a wonderful way to decorate the shelves in your home. You can make it to fit any size of shelf simply by adding or omitting a flag. The kitchen Shelf Bunting would look great in the larder or for trimming the shelves of a large dresser. Why not use the smaller motifs to make matching jam pot lids for your jars of jam and honey?

The Shelf Bunting is so easy to make that you will want to make more. The Sewing Motifs would be ideal for the sewing room; small hearts could be used for bedroom bunting; and, for the nursery, the medium-sized bunny (see Bunny Motifs) is perfect.

Embroidered shelf bunting can brighten up even the most boring of shelves. But I like to use it most when it is unexpected. I still get a thrill every time I open up my larder door to reveal the fabric shelf trims I have made where I store my homemade jams and chutneys.

You will need

- ♡ Two 91.5cm x 15.5cm (36in x 6in) pieces of cream cotton fabric*
- ♡ 91.5cm x 15.5cm (36in x 6in) lightweight iron-on interfacing*
- ♡ Coton à broder: red and taupe, one skein each
- ♡ Propelling pencil
- ♡ 96.5cm x 4cm (38in x 1½in) bias tape**

note: *this is a guide only and your fabric requirements will depend on the length of your shelf; **binding tape can be bought ready-to-use in a variety of colours and a few limited pattern ranges or you can make your own from fabric of your choosing (see Techniques).

Finished size: 80.5cm x 8.8cm (31in x 3½in)

Making the bunting

1. Trace the flag template (see Templates) onto paper. Cut out and stick onto recycled card, and cut out again.

2. Working on the right side of one piece of the fabric with a fine propelling pencil, use the card template to trace around the curves and top line *only* eight times in a straight row. *Do not cut out*.

3. Trace the embroidery motifs onto the flags. Starting and ending with a cupcake, alternate with the small jam jar motif. Place a small motif of your choosing in the jar labels (see Cooking Motifs).

4. Apply the lightweight iron-on interfacing to the wrong side of the bunting and embroider the designs (see opposite).

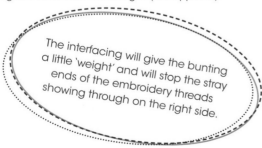

The interfacing will give the bunting a little 'weight' and will stop the stray ends of the embroidery threads showing through on the right side.

5. To mark the curved line on the wrong side of the embroidered fabric, neatly tack along the pencil line. Take the second piece of cotton fabric and pin to the embroidered fabric, right sides together.

6. Sew on the tacked line with a small hand or machine stitch; for great curves, sew as neatly as you can.

7. Cut out the bunting with a scant 6mm (¼in) seam close to the stitching. Use sharp-pointed scissors to snip into the curves of the flag (Fig. 1).

Fig. 1

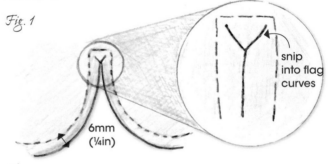

snip into flag curves

6mm (¼in)

8. Turn the bunting the right way out. Use the end of a teaspoon to smooth out the curves of the flags. Press.

9. Using the red thread, sew a running stitch 6mm (¼in) away from the curved edge. Bind the top raw edge with the binding tape to finish.

To make your own custom-made binding as I have done, see Techniques. If you choose to use a check fabric to make the binding it would look better cut on the bias.

Embroidering the bunting

❀ Use the red thread to outline the jam jars with backstitch. Use the taupe thread to add the inner line of the label and define the frill of the jar lid. Use the red and taupe thread for the whipped running stitch braid (1).

❀ Use backstitch for the label motifs of your choosing. Work single stitches for the seeds of the strawberry.

❀ Outline the cupcakes with backstitch. Decorate the cupcake base with lazy daisies, and work single stitches and French knots for the topping decoration.

1

Recipe Book

A fabric-covered notebook is just the thing for keeping special family recipes in. This would make the perfect gift to give a daughter on her wedding day. For basic instructions on making a book cover, see Baby's Record Book in the Baby Bunny chapter. To decorate the Recipe Book I have used the larger jam jar motif to embroider a patch that has been blanket stitched in place. Outline the motif with backstitch, use a blanket stitch for the jar label and whipped running stitch for the string. Individual stitches have been sewn for the seeds on the strawberries and in the jam. A strawberry-embroidered covered button finishes it off perfectly.

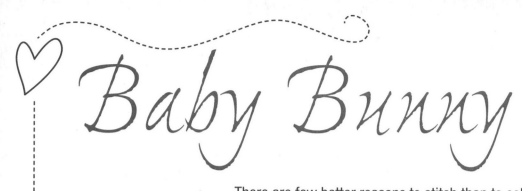

Baby Bunny

There are few better reasons to stitch than to celebrate the arrival of a new baby. And there are few cuter sights than baby rabbits hopping about in the meadows. So, what better motif for the nursery than an adorable baby bunny? The springing bunny motif has been supplied in three sizes. The larger bunny has been used as a wool felt appliqué to decorate the Nursery Cushion. The same motif also inspired me to make the Crib Decoration. The medium-sized bunny is ideal for decorating a notebook to record baby's early days, and scaled down to its smallest size, the bunny makes a great motif for buttons.

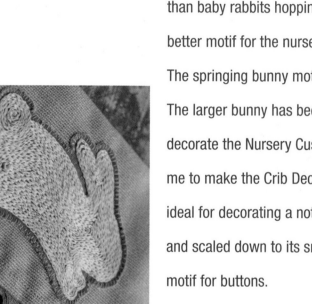

Nursery Cushion

A cushion makes an ideal gift for new parents – it will help them to prop themselves up during those long nighttime feeds. The Nursery Cushion is decorated with a bouncing felt bunny grasping a beautifully embroidered daisy in his paws as he springs through a meadow full of lazy daisy daisies!

The cushion itself is very easy to make – it has a straightforward envelope back and is finished off with a simple ric-rac piping. In fact you may want to fill all the rooms in your home with versions of it. For more inspiration, see the Heart Cushion and the Button Cushion.

This lovely cushion has a timeless feel. For a classic look that would tie in with any colour scheme, I have used a neutral linen for the cushion itself and a creamy white felt for the bunny appliqué. It would look equally lovely, however, made with a cheery gingham and coloured felt, in both pastels and brights. The envelope backing is secured with a hand-embroidered button.

You will need

- ♡ 35.5cm x 91.5cm (14in x 36in) linen
- ♡ 25.5cm (10in) square fusible webbing
- ♡ 20cm x 15.5cm (8in x 6in) cream wool felt
- ♡ Coton à broder: taupe and cream, one skein each
- ♡ One small button
- ♡ 38cm (15in) square cotton mix wadding
- ♡ 1.5m (1⅔yd) medium-width ric-rac
- ♡ Two 29mm self-cover buttons
- ♡ Two 7.5cm (3in) lengths of narrow tape or ribbon
- ♡ 35.5cm x 35.5cm (14in x 14in) cushion pad

Finished size: 35.5cm x 35.5cm (14in x 14in)

Making the cushion top

1. Cut a piece of linen 35.5cm x 35.5cm (14in x 14in) for the cushion top.

2. Use the template (see Baby Bunny Motifs) to trace the large bunny onto the fusible webbing. Roughly cut out and iron onto the back of the wool felt. Carefully cut around the bunny outline and peel off the backing. Position in the centre of the cushion top and iron in place. Using the same method, fix a wool felt circle on the bunny's bottom for the tail. (For more detailed instructions on using fusible webbing see Techniques.)

3. Use carbon paper to transfer the design for the large daisy (see Baby Bunny Motifs) close to the bunny's nose, using the photograph on the previous page as a guide. Make a heart template from card and mark on the body. Embroider the front of the cushion (see Embroidering the cushion top, opposite).

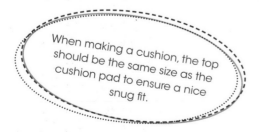

When making a cushion, the top should be the same size as the cushion pad to ensure a nice snug fit.

If using a spray adhesive to secure the wadding, spray the wadding lightly and smooth the fabric on top. Peel off and reposition as necessary. Always use spray adhesive in a well-ventilated area.

4. Take the wadding and pin and tack to the back of the cushion top. Alternatively, use a spray adhesive (see tip above).

5. Embroider a running stitch all the way around the outside edge of the rabbit.

6. Pin the ric-rac to the right side of the cushion top so that the humps of the ric-rac lie on the edge of the cushion. Work your way around all the sides, easing the ric-rac around the corners. Sew down the middle of the braid so that when the cushion is finished and turned through only little half moons will show. As ric-rac frays badly, when you start and finish turn the ric-rac so the raw edges are in the seam allowance. (For more on edging with ric-rac, see Techniques.)

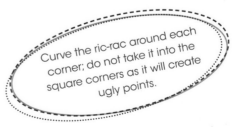

Curve the ric-rac around each corner; do not take it into the square corners as it will create ugly points.

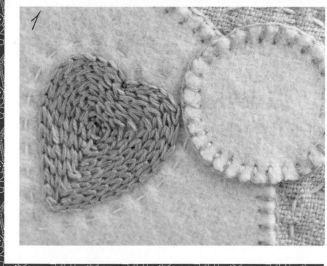

Embroidering the cushion top

❀ Blanket stitch around the outline of the bunny's body and tail. Chain stitch the division between the paws. Satin stitch the nose and sew on a small button for the eye. Sew on some whiskers by taking a small stitch and knotting both ends of the thread close to the felt.

❀ Infill the heart motif with chain stitch and outline with a running stitch (1).

❀ Stitch the middle of the daisy with chain stitch infill, lazy daisy the petals, backstitch the leaves and use whipped running stitch for the stem (2).

❀ Randomly stitch small lazy daisy flowers over the background, finishing each with a French knot in the middle.

Making the cushion back

1. Cut two pieces of linen measuring 35.5cm x 18cm (14in x 7in) and 35.5cm x 25.5cm (14in x 10in). Turn under 6mm (¼in) along one long edge of each rectangle, turn under again and hem.

2. Overlap the two hemmed pieces of fabric until they measure 35.5cm x 35.5cm (14in x 14in).

3. Pin the cushion back to the cushion front, right sides together, and sew around the outside edge on the same line as the ric-rac. Snip the corners and trim the seams. Zig zag over the seams to prevent fraying and turn the right way out.

4. Make two covered buttons using the small rabbit motif (see Small Buttons Motifs) for the embroidery and following the instructions in the Techniques section.

5. Fold the ribbon pieces in half and sew 12.5cm (5in) in from each side on the underside of the top flap to form the button loops. Sew the buttons on the opposite flap so that they line up with the button loops.

Baby's Record Book

This bunny motif is so cute that I just had to use a smaller version of it to decorate a notebook, an ideal place to record those cherished memories of baby's first year of life. This easy-to-make cover has been designed to fit the standard A5 size widely available in supermarkets, stationers and book stores, but it is easily adaptable to fit any book size.

Everyone needs a place to scribble notes, keep lists, record accomplishments, and make plans. Why not make the Traveller's Journal for a globe-trotting friend or the Recipe Book for the chef in the family?

This adaptable cover has fabric flaps to keep the notebook in place, and on the front flap there is a place to store a pen. The cover is decorated with criss-cross braids for a crazy patchwork effect, providing the perfect spaces to fill with embroidery details. A simple ribbon tie is attached to embroidered buttons back and front to prevent the pages from getting grubby between use, and a book marker keeps your place.

You will need

- 50cm x 25.5cm (20in x 10in) linen for cover
- 50cm x 25.5cm (20in x 10in) thin cotton wadding
- Several lengths of decorative tapes, braids and ric-rac of varying widths
- Coton à broder: taupe and cream, one skein each
- 60cm x 25.5cm (22in x 10in) cotton for lining
- 5cm (2in) piece of tape for pen holder
- 30.5cm (12in) piece of narrow tape for book marker
- Four small buttons
- Two 29mm self-cover buttons
- Linen scraps for covering the buttons
- 1m (1⅛yd) of 4cm (1½in) wide binding tape

note: binding tape can be bought ready-to-use in a variety of colours and a few limited pattern ranges or you can make your own from fabric of your choosing.

Finished size: to fit book size 15.5cm x 23cm (6in x 9in) approx.

Making the cover

1. Place the wadding to the wrong side of the cover fabric and pin together.

2. Cut the tapes, braids and ric-rac into different lengths, and lay across the cover fabric at different angles. Hide the ends of the tapes beneath other tapes and off the edges.

3. When you are happy with the layout of the tapes, machine them in place: for the neatest results, sew down the middle of the ric-rac and down either side of the tapes and braids.

4. Roughly fold the fabric around the notebook to check which half is more suitable to use as the front. (The spaces the tapes make will be seen best once the cover is folded around the book, and you can then decide where you would like to embroider the motifs.) Use a fine pencil to transfer the medium-sized bunny and hearts (see Baby Bunny Motifs) to the fabric. Using coton à broder and taking the stitches through to the back of the work, embroider the cover (see right).

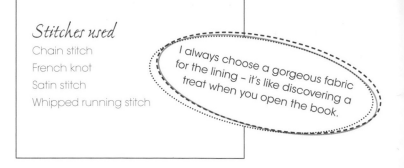

I always choose a gorgeous fabric for the lining – it's like discovering a treat when you open the book.

Embroidering the cover

- Outline the bunny and infill with chain stitch. Add a French knot eye and a few satin stitches for the nose.
- Outline the hearts with a whipped running stitch on the front and a blanket stitch on the back, and sew a small button onto each to decorate.

Making the lining

1. Place the lining fabric and the crazy taped cover wrong sides together. The lining will be bigger than the cover – just match the side seams and pin in place.

2. To make the penholder, fold the 5cm (2in) piece of tape in half and place it in the side seam 2.5cm (1in) down from the top. Repin and sew with a generous 6mm (¼in) seam. Turn the right way out and press; the sides will now be neatly bound.

3. Place the cover around the book and fold the sides evenly over the book boards for the flaps; pin in place and remove the book.

4. To make the bookmarker, pin the narrow decorative tape in the middle of the lining along the top edge. Fold over the tape at the other end and sew a button on either side.

SAFETY NOTE: If the decoration is to be played with substitute satin stitch for the button eyes.

Binding the top and bottom edges

1. Cut two 35.5cm (14in) strips from the binding tape. With the front cover facing you, place one strip along the top edge and sew on with a generous 6mm (¼in) seam leaving 6mm (¼in) overhanging at each end. Sew the other strip to the bottom edge in the same way.

2. Turn the binding over to the cover lining and with double thread slip stitch in place. It is easier if you turn in the ends and sew them in place first before slip stitching along the length of the binding.

3. Make two covered buttons (see Techniques) using the small bunny and heart embroidery motifs (see Small Button Motifs).

4. Cut a 20cm (8in) piece of tape, fold one end over and pin onto the middle edge of the back of the cover. Take one of the covered buttons and sew in place over the tape through to the lining. Sew the other button on the front of the cover. Place the notebook in the cover and close by wrapping the tape around the front button.

Crib Decoration

This simple little hanging decoration uses the same bunny template as the Nursery Cushion and can be made from wool felt leftovers. Cut one bunny and one bunny reversed. Blanket stitch together leaving a small opening at the tummy for stuffing. Fill with polyester toy stuffing and stitch the opening closed. Satin stitch a nose; chain stitch between the ears; embroider a French knot whisker; and backstitch a small heart on the rump. Sew on small black buttons for the eyes. Tie a ribbon in a bow around his neck, and stitch a folded ribbon to the rabbit's back for a hanging loop. Wrap the remaining coton à broder around two fingers and tie very tightly at one end. Cut through the looped threads at the other end. Fluff out and trim the ends neatly. Sew the bobtail to the bunny's bottom.

Garden

The Garden Motifs provide you with a collection of embroidery designs on that most popular of hobbies – gardening. From bees to bird houses, from pea pods to plant pots, there is plenty to choose from. The Gardener's Tidy uses most of them and allows you the opportunity to practise almost all the featured stitches. Alternatively you can choose to use the motifs individually for quick hand-stitched gifts using any of the ideas featured in this book. The seed head or seed packet motif would look great on the front of a gardener's notebook (see the Baby's Record Book for how to make a book cover), the perfect place to jot down what has been grown throughout the year.

Gardener's Tidy

This wall hanging tidy has lots of roomy storage pockets for keeping all your bits and bobs in one place. It has been designed as the perfect canvas for working as many of the gardening motifs as possible, and you will get the chance to try out almost all the featured stitches. But if you prefer, you can choose to embroider just the header and leave the pockets unembroidered.

This project can easily be adapted for the Sew Tidy using the Sewing Motifs (see the Time to Sew chapter). Alternatively, use the Baby Bunny Motifs to run up a carry-all for the nursery.

The Gardener's Tidy will help you keep all your precious seeds and tools in one place. The pockets are surprisingly quick and easy to do, and the addition of a hanging hook means you can take the tidy with you, from the kitchen to the conservatory to the potting shed and back again. Fill it with seed packets, labels, string, dibbers, news articles and colour inspirations from your favourite gardening magazines.

You will need

- 1m (1⅛yd) medium-weight linen
- 50cm x 86.5cm (20in x 34in) fabric for backing
- 60cm (22in) extra wide ric-rac
- Seven 50cm (20in) lengths decorative tapes or ribbons of varying widths
- 2m (2⅛yd) medium-width ric-rac
- Coton à broder thread: cream and taupe, one skein each; red, two skeins
- Red buttons, four large and one medium
- 50cm (20in) narrow tape
- One coat hanger
- 25.5cm (10in) square coordinating cotton fabric
- 10cm (4in) square linen-coloured felt

Finished size: 50cm x 70cm (20in x 28in)

Making the tidy base

1. Cut out a linen rectangle 50cm x 71cm (20in x 28in).

2. Make a paper pattern for the shape of the tidy top (see Templates). Find the middle of the tidy by folding the linen rectangle in half. Using the paper pattern and a pencil, mark the curve at the top of the tidy. This will be cut out eventually, but not just yet. Open out the fabric and mark the centre line with pins.

3. Measure 15.5cm (6in) from the top of the fabric and mark with pins. Transfer the tidy top embroidery designs (see Garden Motifs) above the marked line. Centre the trowel, heart and fork motif and place the pot plant, snail and bee motifs symmetrically on either side using the photograph as a guide.

4. Embroider the motifs for the top of the tidy (see Embroidering the tidy top, opposite).

5. Once the embroidery has been completed cut out the curved shape marked in Step 2.

Stitches used

Backstitch
Running stitch
Whipped running stitch
Chain stitch
Lazy daisy
Stem stitch
Blanket stitch
Satin stitch
Cross stitch
French knot

note: for instructions on transferring the motifs, see Get Ready to Stitch. It is recommended that you make card templates for the larger motifs.

6. With right side facing, place the extra wide ric-rac along the bottom of the linen fabric so that it overlaps the raw edge. Pin in position along the length of the fabric. To avoid getting the ric-rac caught in the seam when you attach the backing, it is important to leave a 1.3cm (½in) at each end ric-rac free. Keep the ric-rac ends out of the way by tucking them back on themselves over the outside edge. Sew down the middle of the ric-rac.

7. Sew the medium-width ric-rac around the remaining edges gently curving around the top corners. This time line up the edge of the ric-rac with the raw edge of the fabric. Sew down the middle of the ric-rac. Take care to position and machine the ric-rac carefully, otherwise when you turn the tidy the right way out in Step 10 the ric-rac will have disappeared. When starting and finishing the ric-rac edging turn back the raw ends, leaving a 6mm (¼in) at each end ric-rac free.

For more detailed instructions on edging with ric-rac see Techniques.

8. To make the casing for the coat hanger, cut a piece of the backing fabric 50cm x 10cm (20in x 4in). Hem along one long edge. Pin to the top of the front of the tidy right sides together; it will not match the curved shape at this stage, but do make sure it covers the whole of the curve.

9. Place the tidy front onto the backing fabric, right sides together. The stitch line from the ric-rac should be visible. Pin the layers together and stitch using the ric-rac stitch line as a guide. Leave a 7.5cm (3in) opening in the middle of one side for turning through.

10. Cut away the excess fabric on the top corners. Trim the seam of the top curve to a scant 6mm (¼in). Carefully snip into the curve on the corners so that the fabric lies flat when turned through. Check your stitching has caught on both sides and turn the right way out. Press well and sew up the opening. Sew a running stitch 6mm (¼in) from the edge all the way around with either a hand or machine stitch. If you choose to sew by hand use an embroidery thread.

Preparing the pockets

1. For the bottom and middle pockets cut two strips of linen fabric 68.6cm x 16.5cm (27in x 6½in).

2. Hem the top edge by turning over 6mm (¼in). Sew a length of decorative tape 6mm (¼in) from the turned over edge, securing along both sides of the tape using a matching thread.

3. Turn the short sides under 6mm (¼in) and press well so they stay in place. Fold the fabric strip in half and press; now fold in half again and press once more. When the fabric is opened out it will have three visible pressed lines which define the four pocket areas.

4. In the middle of these pocket areas, transfer and stitch a motif of your choice using the Garden Motifs. For the bottom row, from left to right, the bird house, gardening glove, watering can and beehive have been chosen and transferred onto the fabric using cardboard templates. For the middle row the seed packet motif has been repeated on each pocket using the same transfer method. Each seed packet is decorated with a different fruit and vegetable motif, transferred using carbon paper.

Embroidering the tidy top

❀ Stitch the outline of the tools and the heart with backstitch.

❀ Infill the tools and the heart with a chain stitch. Outline the heart with a stem stitch, then a running stitch; add a backstitch shoot growing out of the heart topped with two lazy daisies for the seedling.

❀ Backstitch the outline of the snail body and the flower pot, and the whole of the bee. Add French knots for the eyes of the bee and the snail.

❀ Satin stitch a heart onto the flower pot and three cross stitches along its rim. Stitch three lazy daisy flowers with backstitch stems in the pot (1).

5. Embroider the motifs for the middle and bottom pockets of the tidy (see below and opposite).

6. The bird house pocket is specially designed to keep garden string tidy. To make the hole to pull the garden string through, sew a small circle of running stitches. Snip the fabric in the middle of the circle from the centre out to the edge a couple of times Oversew the edges of the snipped fabric with tiny straight stitches worked close together. Finish off with a row of backstitch close to the edge of the circle to neaten things up.

7. For the shallower top pockets, cut a strip of linen fabric measuring 68.6cm x 12.5cm (27in x 5in). Prepare as for the bottom and middle pockets (see Step 3).

8. To decorate the top pockets, cut four 5cm (2in) squares of cotton fabric and attach to the middle of each section using fusible webbing (see Techniques). Cut small circles from the felt and attach to the square cotton patches in the same way. Blanket stitch around the edges of the cotton patches and the felt circles, then embroider the flowers in the middle of the circles using lazy daisy, running stitch, French knots and satin stitch.

Embroidering the middle pockets

❧ Sew the outline of the seed packets and the vegetables with backstitch.

❧ Sew the labels with a blanket stitch.

❧ Sew the fold of the seed packet flap with running stitch.

❧ Sew the seeds spilling out of the packets using a variety of stitches, from left to right on the finished tidy, French knots, small lazy daisies, tiny dots and running stitches.

Embroidering the bottom pockets

❀ Backstitch the outline of the bird house. Infill the roof and table with chain stitch. Chain stitch the outside of the post. See Preparing the pockets, Step 6 for making the entrance hole.

❀ Backstitch around the outline of the gardening glove. Infill the cuff with rows of chain stitch. Cut a heart from cotton fabric and use fusible webbing to attach it to the centre of the glove. Blanket stitch around the edge of the heart. Finish by sewing individual cross stitches all over the glove (1).

❀ Backstitch around the outline of the watering can and the flower stem. Highlight the handle, base and rim of the watering can with a running stitch. Blanket stitch the label. Sew the flower and leaves with a lazy daisy, and a French knot in the centre (2).

❀ Backstitch the outline of the hive, the hive entrance and the feet. Satin stitch the hive entrance and feet. Define the hive sections with a running stitch. Sew the bee with backstitch and add French knots for the eyes (3).

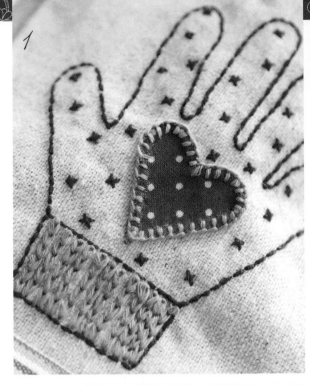

Sewing on the pockets

1. Use a pencil and ruler to draw a centred 46cm (18in) line 2.5cm (1in) up from the bottom of the tidy. Divide the line into four equal sections of 11.5cm (4½in).

2. Place the raw edge of the bottom pocket onto the drawn line. Pin the left-hand side seam at the start of the line. Taking care to keep the bottom of the pocket straight on the marked line, pin the first pressed line onto the first marked section, the second pressed line onto the second marked section, and the third pressed line onto the third marked section. The right-hand side seam will line up with the end of the line (Fig. 1).

Fig. 1

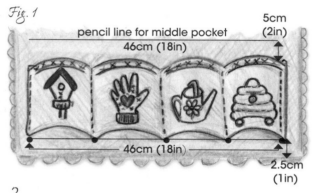

pencil line for middle pocket

46cm (18in)

5cm (2in)

46cm (18in)

2.5cm (1in)

3. Re-pin the pocket lines in place so you can sew over the pins. Machine stitch in place on the pressed lines, reinforcing the top divisions of the pocket with a few back stitches.

4. Tuck and fold the excess material in each pocket equally and pin at the bottom. The rest of the folds will fall into place naturally. Sew the raw lower edge of the pockets onto the backing to hold the folds in place (Fig. 2).

Fig. 2

5. Pin and sew a piece of decorative tape or ribbon over the raw edge at the base of the pockets. Stitch along both edges of the tape, starting with the edge of the tape closest to the pockets to make sure all the raw edges are caught in.

6. Repeat this process with the middle and top pocket rows, positioning the middle pocket line 5cm (2in) above the bottom pocket and the top pocket line 7.5cm (3in) above the top of the middle pocket.

7. Sew a large button 5cm (2in) above each pocket in the middle row. Cut 12.5cm (5in) lengths of ribbon, one for each pocket, fold in half and sew centrally inside the top of each pocket. Fasten the ribbon loops around the buttons. Attach the medium button in the corner of the bird house pocket and use this to wind the end of the garden string on to keep it from unravelling.

8. Finally, you can let free rein to your creativity, adding extra stitches, embroidery motifs or buttons to the tidy. For example, I have added lazy daisy flowers to the bottom of the tidy and a buzzing bee trail in running stitch above the bottom pocket row.

To make the hanger

1. Place the coat hanger into the casing at the back. Cut a small hole for the hanger hook to go through and neaten with blanket stitch. Sew the casing opening closed.

2. Cut a strip of thin fabric 5cm x 15cm (2in x 6in) and fold it in half along its width. Turn in the seams along the top and sides; hand stitch together with a running stitch, but do not fasten off. Slip the fabric tube over the hook of the hanger and gather up. When all the fabric is gathered fasten off onto the back of the tidy.

Gardener's Apron

This would make an ideal gift for a gardening friend and the addition of the large red button between the two pocket sections is useful for holding lengths of string for tying in roses. The large pockets of the tea towel apron are perfect for the large seed head motifs (see the Cook's Apron for making up instructions). Cut two pieces of linen fabric for the embroideries 15cm (6in) square. Transfer the seed head motif using carbon paper reversing the stalk of one of the seed heads so that they both face inwards. Embroider the designs with stem stitch, running stitch, chain stitch and French knots.

Buttons

Button collecting has always been a passion of mine, and I am especially keen on pearl buttons. On a cold and rainy afternoon I like nothing better than to sort through my button box, and even my children join in the fun. Some pearl buttons are so very beautifully engraved, but, as they are increasingly difficult to find in second-hand shops or at car boot sales, I decided to make a few of my own – out of felt! It all started by doodling my favourite buttons. I thought the design would make a nice embroidery, then I had a go at turning it into a felt appliqué; from there, I made the Button Cushion which led directly onto the Button Bracelet. Isn't it amazing where playing with a few old buttons can lead you?

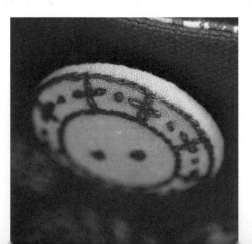

Button Bag

For such a simply made bag, this elegant shopper really couldn't be bettered in its design or finish. Made from a durable cotton fabric, it has a stylish coordinating lining, a wide, comfortable handle included in the seam, and a tidy square bottom so that it sits neatly on the shop counter ready to be packed with your goodies.

Best of all, it has a delightful button collage embroidered on the front and is secured with a button embroidered with a button! The button collage appears again on the Button Cushion worked as a felt appliqué.

This chic carrier can be made in lots of different sizes, from very small to very large. To give you an idea of just how adaptable it can be, take a look at the cute Little Sew Bag in the Time to Sew chapter. After all, a girl can never have enough bags!

You will need

- 42cm x 75cm (16½in x 29½in) cotton for main fabric
- 42cm x 75cm (16½in x 29½in) coordinating cotton for lining fabric
- 1m (1¼yd) webbing tape for the handle
- 25.5cm x 75cm (10in x 29½in) medium-weight iron-on interfacing
- Coton à broder: taupe and salmon pink, one skein each
- 48mm self-cover button
- Popper fastener

note: if your lining fabric is striped like mine, to ensure the stripes run in the right direction, cut the fabric following the grain, i.e. the direction of the stripes.

Finished size: 70cm x 50cm (28in x 20in)

Making the bag

1. Trace the button collage design (see Button Motifs) onto the main fabric, positioning it 5cm (2in) down from the top edge.

2. Iron the interfacing onto the middle of the wrong side of the main fabric. Embroider the button collage design (see opposite).

3. Fold the main fabric in half right sides together and sew along either side. Repeat for the lining fabric, but this time leave a 7.5cm (3in) opening on one seam (Fig. 1). Press.

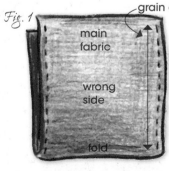

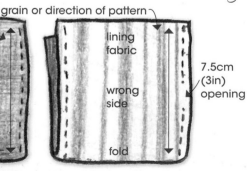

Fig. 1

grain or direction of pattern

main fabric

wrong side

fold

lining fabric

wrong side

fold

7.5cm (3in) opening

Stitches used

Backstitch

Lazy daisy

Satin stitch

Running stitch

Herringbone stitch

French knot

note: use dressmaker's carbon paper to transfer the embroidery design.

4. 'Sugar bag' the main fabric by squashing the side seams onto the bottom (Fig. 2). Measure 5cm (2in) in from each point and sew a straight line across. Repeat for the lining, but trim off the points to 6mm (¼in) and turn the right way out.

Fig. 2

wrong side

5. Pin the handle over each side seam on the main fabric bag. Put the lining into the main fabric bag (Fig. 3); pin and sew all the way around the top edge. Sew twice over the handles to secure.

Fig. 3

lining right side

handle

wrong side

6. Turn the right way out through the opening in the lining and slip stitch to close. Press. Sew on the popper fastening inside the bag.

7. Decorate the bag by embroidering the self-cover button (see Techniques) and sew in place to camouflage your fastening.

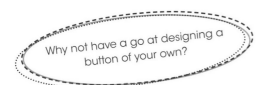

Why not have a go at designing a button of your own?

For a smaller bag

To make a smaller version of the bag (see the Little Sew Bag in the Time to Sew chapter) you will need two pieces of coordinating linen measuring 25.5cm x 50cm (10in x 20in) and a linen strip measuring 40.5cm x 5cm (16in x 5in) for the handle. Sew the handle along its length right sides together. Turn the right way out and press so the seam is in the centre. Sew a piece of decorative tape over the seam. Make up the bag as above and when pinning the handle into the main bag (Step 5), make sure the decorative tape side is facing down. To close, the bag handle is threaded through fastening loops. Cut two 15.5cm (6in) lengths of 2.5cm (1in) tape. Fold in half and pin to the centre front and centre back of the main bag before inserting the lining.

Embroidering the button collage

❀ Refer to the button collage motif (see Buttons Motifs) to identify the buttons.

❀ **Button 1:** Backstitch the circle, satin stitch the buttonholes, and add the lazy daisies.

❀ **Button 2:** Blanket stitch the outer circle, stem stitch the inner circle, and satin stitch the buttonholes.

❀ **Button 3:** Backstitch the outer and inner circles, lazy daisy the border, use backstitch to cross hatch the centre, and satin stitch the buttonholes.

❀ **Button 4:** Backstitch the outer and inner circles, lazy daisy the flower border and satin stitch the buttonholes.

❀ **Button 5:** Backstitch the outer circle and running stitch just inside. Lazy daisy the petals and satin stitch the buttonholes. Embroider the inner circle with an upside down blanket stitch.

❀ **Button 6:** Backstitch the outer circle and running stitch just inside. Work French knots for the buttonholes.

❀ **Button 7:** Backstitch the circles. Herringbone the border. Satin stitch the buttonholes.

❀ **Buttons 8 & 9:** Backstitch the button design and satin stitch the buttonholes.

❀ **Button 10:** Chain stitch the outer circle and stem stitch the two inner circles. Backstitch the radials between the inner and middle circle. Add French knots around the border.

Button Bracelet

For many years I have been making and designing button jewellery. My collection of buttons has two categories: those buttons suitable for making jewellery – nice colours, not too rare, sometimes handmade – and those buttons that are just so special that they must stay in the tin. But I can use my special button collection to inspire my felt button designs.

Each 'button' measures 3cm (1⅛in) and is made from wool felt and embroidered with coton à broder. Eight buttons make a bracelet to fit the average wrist, but a ninth button design is provided should you need it.

You can make the lovely felt buttons any size you choose and substitute them for real buttons. I used a large felt button to fasten the back of the Heart Cushion (see the Hearts chapter). The Button Bracelet gives you the perfect opportunity to design some buttons of your own using the stitch guide for inspiration.

You will need

- ♡ Two 20cm (8in) squares wool felt
- ♡ 20cm (8in) square fusible webbing
- ♡ Coton à broder: taupe, one skein
- ♡ Popper for fastening

Finished size: diameter of each button 3cm (1⅛in). The length of the bracelet will depend on the size of your wrist.

Making the bracelet

1. Transfer the bracelet buttons (see Buttons Motifs) onto one wool felt square. Use the fusible webbing to stick together the wool felt squares.

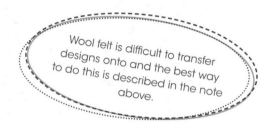

Wool felt is difficult to transfer designs onto and the best way to do this is described in the note above.

2. Cut out the circles and blanket stitch the two layers of felt together around the outside edges of the button.

3. Embroider the buttons (see right).

4. Overlap each button by 6mm (¼in) and sew together on the wrong side. For the fastening, sew the ball half of the popper to the top of one end of the bracelet and the socket half to the bottom of the other end.

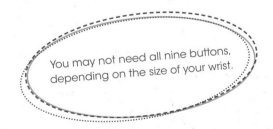

You may not need all nine buttons, depending on the size of your wrist.

Stitches used

Backstitch
Lazy daisy
French knot
Cross stitch

note: use card template to transfer the button circle and dressmaker's carbon paper to transfer the detail of each design.

Embroidering the buttons

❀ Refer to the bracelet buttons motifs (see Buttons Motifs) to identify the buttons. When working the embroidery do not stitch right through to the back of the buttons.

❀ **Button 1:** Backstitch the inner circle and lazy daisy the petals.

❀ **Button 2:** Backstitch the three circles

❀ **Button 3:** Lazy daisy the petals.

❀ **Button 4:** Backstitch.

❀ **Button 5:** Lazy daisy the petals and backstitch the inner circle.

❀ **Button 6:** Lazy daisy the flowers and French knot the dots.

❀ **Button 7:** Backstitch the inner circle and the radials.

❀ **Button 8:** Cross stitch.

❀ **Button 9:** Backstitch.

❀ French knot all the buttonholes.

Button Cushion

The button collage design has been used as wool felt appliqué to decorate the front of a cushion. Trace off the design onto fusible webbing, cut out and fuse onto the front cushion fabric. Embroider the detail of the design and make up as a cushion following the instructions for the Heart Cushion in the Hearts chapter.

♥ Travel

All through the year we dream of packing our bags and taking a holiday far away from the routines of daily life. Whether you imagine a vibrant city break or fantasize about getting away from it all on a desert island, stitching the Travel Motifs will keep you busy while you countdown the days to your next trip, and the projects will prove very useful when your holiday finally arrives. Avoid the desperate last-minute search for your passport by keeping it safe in a dedicated folder that's large enough for all your travel documents but sufficiently compact to slip into your hand luggage. Other traveller's essentials include a distinctive Luggage Tag and a Traveller's Journal.

Documents Folder

A fabric folder is a very useful thing, and the size of the one I have designed is adaptable for any number of uses. The A5-size shown is ideal for keeping passport and travel documents all in one place, and a personalised tag on the front flap ensures each traveller's papers are easy to identify.

The travel document folder makes the perfect present for gap year students, but simply substitute the motif to create a whole range of practical gifts. For a cook's recipe folder, choose a cupcake, and for a sewing pattern file for stitcher's, select the sewing machine.

The A5 fabric folder is simple to size up for larger items, and, to keep fragile objects safe, you can replace the interfacing with wadding applied with a little spray adhesive. Suitably padded it would make the ideal container for a digital notebook or a laptop.

You will need

- 28cm x 46cm (11in x 18in) cotton for main fabric
- 28cm x 46cm (11in x 18in) cotton for lining fabric
- 48cm (19in) medium-width ric-rac
- 28cm x 46cm (11in x 18in) fusible interfacing
- 5cm (2in) decorative tape
- 14cm x 10cm (5½in x 4in) linen for embroidery patch
- Stranded cotton (floss): red and taupe
- 10cm x 6.5cm (4in x 2½in) wool felt
- Small button
- Popper

note: for a netbook folder – fabric size 30.5cm x 60cm (12in x 22in), ric-rac length 50cm (20in); for an A4 folder – fabric size 35.5cm x 60cm (14in x 22in), ric-rac length 60cm (22in).

Finished size: 19cm x 28cm (7⅜in x 11in)

Making the folder

1. Place the main and lining fabrics on top of each other. Measuring 10cm (4in) down from the top edge make a small snip through both fabrics on either side.

2. Using a pencil and a tea plate, mark a curved shape in the top left-hand corner of the fabrics, from the top edge to the snipped fabric (see Fig. 1). Repeat on the right-hand corner. Cut out the corner shapes.

Fig. 1

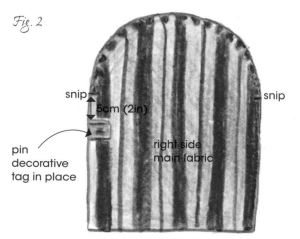

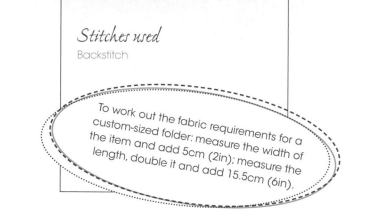

To work out the fabric requirements for a custom-sized folder: measure the width of the item and add 5cm (2in); measure the length, double it and add 15.5cm (6in).

3. Sew a strip of ric-rac along the top curve of the main fabric only, starting and stopping at the snips. Make sure you line the ric-rac up with the edge of the fabric, and sew down the middle of the ric-rac. To add a decorative tag fold the tape in half and place in the left-hand seam about 5cm (2in) from the snip (Fig. 2).

Fig. 2

pin decorative tag in place

snip · 5cm (2in) · snip

right side main fabric

4. To add a little weight to your folder for a crisper finish, iron a layer of interfacing onto the wrong side of the lining fabric.

5. Place the main and lining fabrics together with right sides facing, and pin the top and bottom edges.

6. Sew the top edge along the same line as the ric-rac. Sew along the bottom edge with a 6mm (¼in) seam.

Luggage Tag

Cut a large tag from red felt. Cut out the centre and the slit, and blanket stitch. Fold a 33cm x 23cm (13in x 9in) strip of linen fabric in half; press. Draw round the tag onto the linen and sew along this line leaving a small gap. Trim close to the stitching and diagonally at the corners. Turn through, press, and sew closed. Transfer the plane motif; backstitch the outline, lazy daisy the propeller and satin stitch the windows. Sew a running stitch border. Blanket stitch the curved edge of the linen tag only. Pin the felt tag to the unembroidered side of the linen tag; blanket stitch together continuing around the curved end of the felt tag only. Fold a 20cm (8in) tape in half and stitch to the linen tag to align with the slit in the felt tag. Slip in a piece of clear plastic. To close, thread the tape through the slit..

Traveller's Journal

No intrepid voyager should leave home without a notebook to record his or her adventures. This would make the perfect gift for students about to set off on a gap year. The basic instructions are the same as for the Baby's Record Book in the Baby Bunny chapter, but this time the decoration has been kept simple. Choose a durable fabric and transfer the motif directly onto the cover. The Eiffel Tower motif has been stitched in backstitch with a single strand of stranded cotton (floss) for a subtle effect, and, for a decorative finish a medium-width ric-rac has been hand-stitched to the book's spine.

7. Pick up the lining and fold the main fabric right up to the snip. Sew the main fabric side seams right up to the snip. Fasten off securely. Now sew both side seams of the lining fabric up to the snip, leaving a sufficient gap for turning through the right way (Fig. 3).

Fig. 3

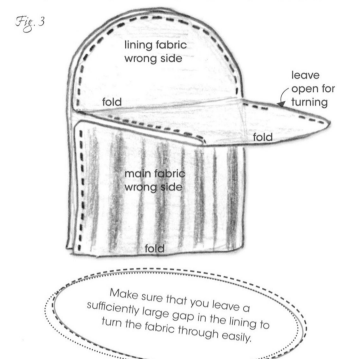

lining fabric wrong side

leave open for turning

fold

fold

main fabric wrong side

fold

Make sure that you leave a sufficiently large gap in the lining to turn the fabric through easily.

8. Trim diagonally across the bottom corners of the lining fabric and around the top curve. Turn the right way out and push the lining into the folder (Fig.4). Press.

Fig. 4

push lining into folder

9. Transfer the suitcase motif (see Travel Motifs) to the linen patch and embroider (see below). Press under a 6mm (¼in) seam all the way around and stitch to the back of the folder with a blanket stitch.

10. Cut a small luggage tag from wool felt (see Travel Motifs). Transfer the recipient's initials from the Alphabet Motifs to a scrap of linen fabric that is larger than the inner aperture of the luggage tag. Position the luggage tag on the front flap of the folder with the linen beneath it, and sew on using blanket stitch all the way around the inner aperture and the outer edge. Add a button for decoration. Secure the folder with a popper sewn under the flap.

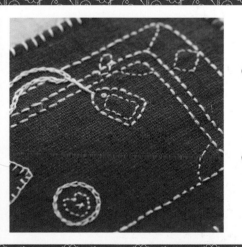

Embroidering the back cover patch

🌼 Using two strands, backstitch the main shape of the suitcase and the outline of the luggage tag. Chain stitch the handle. Blanket stitch the rectangular label and chain stitch the circular label.

🌼 Using one strand, backstitch the details of the suitcase (the clasps, the corners and the square label) the luggage tag label, and the heart in the circular sticker.

Christmas

I have always loved the festivities and celebrations of the Christmas period. It starts quite early at my house with the baking of the cake and the making of the Christmas pudding. Then there's the tradition of going as a family to select the perfect tree from our local farm, where we enjoy mulled wine and homemade biscuits and post our Christmas wish on the wishing tree. But best of all is the unpacking of all the decorations I have been stitching throughout the year to decorate not just the tree, but all around the house. This year will be no exception with gift tags for the presents, heart garlands for the mantel, stars for the tree, and, my favourite, the Christmas wreath for the door.

Christmas Wreath

This door wreath is made from a simple wire base decorated with fabric rags and felt stars and hearts. It's a great way to use up those linen leftovers from a year's worth of stitching projects. My children help with the tearing up of the fabric and the tying of the knots. The hearts and stars take just a couple of evenings to complete.

The wreath would look great on any internal door, or use it to decorate the feature wall in the living room. For coordinated Christmas decorations, make heart garlands and hanging stars for the tree.

The base of this gorgeous Christmas wreath is a wire coat hanger shaped into a circle. The hanger's handle is useful for hanging the finished garland. But no one would guess what lies beneath the mass of linen rags. Be warned, thicker fabrics do not work with this project and a lot of material is needed if you want your wreath to be voluptuous.

You will need

- 1.5m (1¾yd) 120cm (42in) wide dress-weight cotton fabric
- Wire coat hanger shaped into a circle
- Two 33cm x 40.5cm (13in x 16in) pieces of white felt
- Coton à broder: red and taupe, one skein each
- Polyester stuffing
- 23cm x 15cm (9in x 6in) red felt
- Three small pearl buttons
- Twelve small red heart buttons

Finished size: wreath diameter approx. 30.5cm (12in)

Making the wreath base

1. Cut off the selvedge edges of the fabric. Snip along the edge of the fabric every 4cm (1½in) and tear into strips. Put one strip aside.

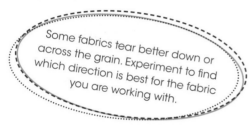

Some fabrics tear better down or across the grain. Experiment to find which direction is best for the fabric you are working with.

2. Pull off the stray threads and cut the remaining strips into 12.5cm (5in) lengths. This is a crucial measurement – too long a strip will result in limp rags, too short a strip will result in no rags at all. Stack the strips up and cut through a load at one time. The last thing you want to do is to cut them too neatly.

3. Tie each strip onto the coat hanger with a single knot and push all the rags up tight to get as many strips on as possible.

4. Take the remaning strip, fold it in half wrong sides together along its length, and turn under a seam allowance along both long edges and along one end. Using double sewing thread to match the fabric, cast on securely and sew a running stitch across one end and down the folded side to make a tube. Do not cast off.

5. Thread the strip over the hook of the hanger and pull up the gathering stitches. Fasten off onto the nearest rag knot.

Making the stars and hearts

1. Trace off the three star templates (see Christmas Motifs) onto card and use to draw the shapes onto the white felt. Do not cut out at this stage as, if you do, the star shape will be distorted when embroidering.

2. Transfer the embroidery motifs using carbon paper. This may prove a bit difficult as the felt is spongy; if it is a problem, make card templates of the birds and holly and trace around. Take care to position the embroidery designs correctly as the star has a top and bottom, which are very easy to get muddled up.

3. Embroider the designs (see Embroidering the felt stars, opposite) then cut out the stars. Place the stars onto the second white felt square, pin in place, then cut around each star for its backing.

4. Keeping the pins in place, blanket stitch all the way around each star leaving a 2.5cm (1in) gap. Gently stuff with polyester stuffing and then continue stitching to close the gap. Remove pins.

5. Cut six hearts from red felt (see Christmas Motifs). Blanket stitch pairs of hearts together around the edges and stuff.

6. To finish off the stars, sew on some small red buttons to represent holly berries. To finish off the hearts, sew a small pearl button to the middle of each, right through to the back. Sew the hearts and stars onto the wreath using the photograph as a guide.

Embroidering the felt stars

❀ Backstitch the outline of the birds and the holly leaves.

❀ Add lines of running stitch to the centre of the holly leaves.

❀ Stitch French knots for the birds' eyes.

❀ The stars are embroidered by working two cross stitches on top of each other.

Christmas Tree Decorations

The stars can be made individually to hang on the Christmas tree. Sew loops of thread onto the stars for hanging. For an extra garland make six red hearts. Decorate the centre of each with a star (embroider two cross stitches on top of each other) and add a thread hanging loop at the top of each. Take about a metre (yard) of decorative tape, turn under at either end and neaten with a small button. Sew little heart buttons along the length of the tape at equal distances from each other, and use these buttons to hang the felt hearts from. If you prefer, you can alternate the hearts with stars.

Present Tags

Make your Christmas gifts even more special with these beautiful embroidered scenes of festive decorations each displayed within a felt tag aperture. They are a joy to stitch and so versatile to use.

Attach them to the presents beneath the tree, send in place of a card to friends and family far away, thread several along a decorative tape for a mantle decoration, or hang individually from the branches of your Christmas tree. The choice is yours.

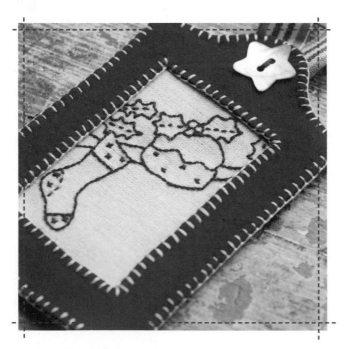

I have designed four festive scenes for you to embroider to make present tags to make your gifts extra special this year. I was particularly pleased with the mother-of-pearl star buttons I found and I used these to hide the stitches used to attach the ribbon loops to the completed present tags.

You will need

- ♥ 20cm (8in) square calico
- ♥ 30.5cm x 40.5cm (12in x 16in) red felt
- ♥ 20cm (8in) square fusible webbing
- ♥ Stranded cotton (floss): red, one skein
- ♥ Coton à broder: taupe, one skein
- ♥ 60cm (24in) decorative tape
- ♥ Four star buttons

Finished size: 7.5cm x 12cm (3in x 4¾in)

1. Cut out four 7.5cm x 10cm (3in x 4in) rectangles from the calico. Trace the four scenes (see Christmas Motifs) onto the calico and embroider (see Embroidering the scenes, opposite).

The calico should be easy to see the design through to trace off.

2. Using the present tag template (see Christmas Motifs) cut out eight gift tags from the red felt. Cut the centre aperture from four of the tags for the front of the gift tags.

3. Cut out four rectangles from the fusible webbing that are just a little smaller than the embroidered calico rectangles. Place the rough side of the webbing onto the back of the embroidery and iron to fix. Peel off the paper and position the stitched work onto a felt gift tag back. Check the position by placing the gift tag front over the embroidery. Once you are happy with the embroidery position, iron in place. Using the coton à broder, blanket stitch around the outside of the tag first, then around the aperture.

4. Cut the tape into four 15cm (6in) lengths. Cut both ends of the tapes at a 45-degree angle. Fold the tape in half, cross over the ends and stitch in place to the back of the tag. Sew the star button on the front of the tag.

Stitches used

Backstitch
Running stitch
Cross stitch
French knot
Lazy daisy

Cutting smaller fusible webbing rectangles ensures that there is no danger of sticking them to the iron or the ironing board.

Embroidering the scenes

❀ Embroider the design using two strands of stranded cotton (floss).

❀ Backstitch the outline of the scenes and add a running stitch line to the centre of the holly leaves to add detail.

❀ **Scene 1:** Stitch a line of running stitch around the inside of the star and embroider two cross stitches, one on top of the other, for the centre star.

❀ **Scene 2:** Add French knot detailing to the wreath and for the bird's eye. Work a double cross stitch star within the star as for Scene 1. Stitch a lazy daisy in the middle of the bauble.

❀ **Scene 3:** Stitch a line of running stitch to detail the edge of the bell, and French knots to the centre of the heart and for the bird's eye.

❀ **Scene 4:** Work individual cross stitches to add detailing to the stocking and Christmas pudding.

Step-by-step instructions are provided in the project chapters to enable you to make the beautiful things featured. But when you need a little more help, the more detailed advice in this section will clarify some key techniques.

Using a sewing machine

A sewing machine will produce much stronger seams and a more uniform, professional result than hand stitching when making up the projects. It is well worth taking a little time to get to know your sewing machine better. The best way to do this is to read the instruction manual that came with it, and to test stitch on the fabrics you have selected for your chosen project.

The commonest problems you are likely to encounter are poor tension and missing stitches and these are usually easy to solve. *Poor tension* If the stitching on the back and the front of the fabric is not perfectly balanced, check that you have threaded the machine correctly and that the bobbin you are using is the right one (there are commonly two sizes) and that it has been inserted the correct way. *Missing stitches* When was the last time you changed the needle? A needle needs to be changed after every major project. Always use a good-quality needle, size 80 (12) or 90 (14).

Detail of the envelope back of the Baby Bunny Nursery Cushion.

To get the best from your machine, keep it well maintained. Use the special brushes provided to clean away the dust and fabric residue that builds up after each project, paying particular attention to the bobbin and its casing. If the manual advises it, give your machine a light oil. Make sure you use oil that is specifically designed for sewing machines. If these general maintenance tips do not solve the problems you are experiencing, seek the advice of your local service engineer.

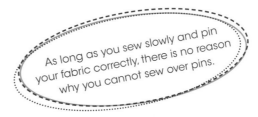

As long as you sew slowly and pin your fabric correctly, there is no reason why you cannot sew over pins.

Working with fusible webbing

Fusible webbing is used when you want to appliqué one piece of fabric to another, for example the wool felt bunny to the Nursery Cushion and the red heart to the top of the Sewing Tidy. It is an iron-on fabric adhesive that can be purchased in a roll or in pre-cut pieces and it looks like paper. One side can be drawn on (so you can trace the motif you want) and the other has a thin membrane of glue that melts when heated by an iron, to attach the two fabrics together. To use fusible webbing, follow these simple step-by-step instructions.

1. Trace the motif you want onto the paper (smooth) side of the fusible webbing. Cut roughly around the drawn motif rather than following the drawn line accurately at this stage.

2. Iron the fusible webbing onto the wrong side of the appliqué fabric making sure that the fusible webbing is glue (rough) side down. The glue on the back of the fusible webbing melts when heated so be very careful to iron the paper side or else it will stick to your iron.

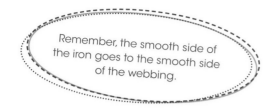

Remember, the smooth side of the iron goes to the smooth side of the webbing.

3. Once the fusible webbing has been attached to the appliqué fabric you can cut out the motif accurately on the drawn line.

4. Carefully peel off the backing paper and position the appliqué motif onto the fabric it is to be applied to. Iron to fix in place.

Edging with ric-rac braid

I love ric-rac braid and often use it to edge my projects as on the Gardener's Tidy and the Nursery Cushion. Both extra wide ric-rac and medium ric-rac make a great edging embellishment, but they are applied slightly differently.

This corner detail of the Gardener's Tidy shows the medium and extra wide ric-rac edging off beautifully.

Edging with medium ric-rac

It is important to position and machine the ric-rac carefully to prevent the humps of the ric-rac from disappearing when the project is turned the right way out. Working on the right side of the fabric, line up the edge of the ric-rac with the raw edge of the fabric. Tack in place by machine stitching down the middle of the ric-rac. When starting and finishing the edging keep the ends out of the way by tucking them back on themselves to leave the seam allowance ric-rac free (Fig. 1).

Fig. 1

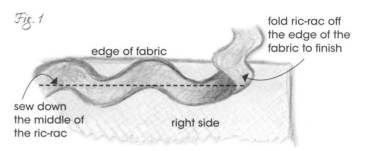

fold ric-rac off the edge of the fabric to finish

edge of fabric

sew down the middle of the ric-rac

right side

Edging with extra wide ric-rac

Working on the right side of the fabric, place the extra wide ric-rac so that it overlaps the raw edges of the fabric as shown in Fig. 2 and pin in place. Sew a line of machine stitching 6mm (¼in) from the fabric edge down the middle of the ric-rac braid. When starting and finishing the edging keep the ends out of the way by tucking them back on themselves to leave the seam allowance ric-rac free (see Fig. 1).

Fig. 2

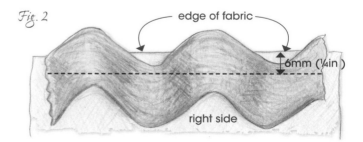

edge of fabric

6mm (¼in)

right side

Custom-made binding

Bindings decorate and finish a raw edge at the same time. Binding tape can be bought ready-to-use in a variety of colours and a few limited pattern ranges, or you can make your own from fabric of your choosing. To make your own binding, cut 4cm (1½in) wide strips across the width of the fabric and join them together with a 6mm (¼in) seam, open out the seam and press.

I used a custom-made binding for the Heart Blanket. To make 4cm (1½in) wide binding strips for this project you will need ¼m (¼yd) of your chosen fabric. Lay the binding along one side, matching the raw edges. Turn under and pin 6mm (¼in) at both ends. Sew using a generous 6mm (¼in) seam. Fold the binding over to the back, turn under a 6mm (¼in) seam and slip stitch in place.

If you are using store-bought binding strips, the long edges are already turned under. Open out one folded edge of the strip. Lay the raw edges together and sew along the first fold line. Turn the binding over to the back of the blanket and slip stitch in place. Ready-made binding is usually sold by its finished size, so for the Heart Blanket you would buy a 2.5cm (1in) binding

Detail of bias bound edging of the Shelf Bunting.

Making bias binding

If you choose to use a check fabric to make the binding, as I have done for the Shelf Bunting, it must be cut on the bias. If you do not cut checks or stripes on the bias you will only see a straight line of the fabric design and this may not be straight, which never looks very good

Using a square or rectangle of fabric, take a corner and fold it at a 45-degree angle (this is half a square from one corner to the opposite corner) and press. Cut the folded edge carefully. Mark and cut the remainder fabric into 4cm (1½in) strips.

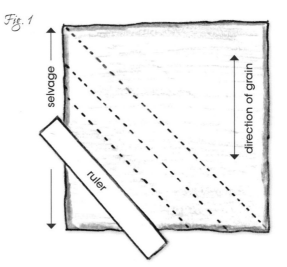

Fig. 1

selvage

direction of grain

ruler

To join the strips it is easier to cut the ends straight. Lay the ends of the strips on top of each other right sides together, making sure the top strip overlaps the bottom strip by 6mm (¼in) . Sew from the top left-hand corner to the bottom right-hand corner, trim the seams to 6mm (¼in) (Fig. 2) and press open. Use as custom-made binding.

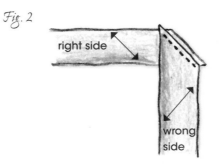

Fig. 2

right side

wrong side

Making covered buttons

There is nothing better to embellish your project than a hand-embroidered button. I have used these time and time again on the projects in this book and I have even included lots of small button designs (pictured above) in the Motifs section.

To make a covered button you will need a self-cover button. These are available in plastic and metal in a range of different sizes. I have used 22mm, 29mm, 39mm and 48mm, but if you cannot get the exact same size button, use the nearest to it.

1. Cut out a circle of fabric approximately 1.3cm (½in) bigger than the self-cover button all the way around. Embroider the design onto the fabric circle as instructed in the project.

2. Sew a row of gathering (running) stitches around the outside edge of the circle (Fig.1). Make sure that you fasten on the thread securely and that you use double thread.

Fig. 1

3. Put the button in the middle of the circle, pull up the gathered stitches tightly and fasten off securely (Fig.2).

Fig. 2

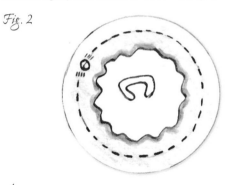

4. Put the button back over the shank and push firmly into place. If you are using a thicker fabric, it can help to put a cotton reel over the shank and push hard with the ball of your hand (Fig.3).

Fig. 3

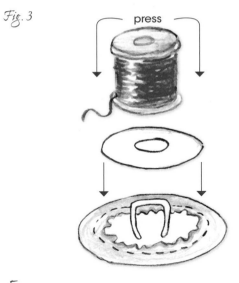

press

5. For a decorative finish, blanket stitch around the edges of the covered button.

Metal buttons have teeth that you can push your fabric under for a more secure fit.

# Motifs

note: the motifs and templates in this book are the actual size you will need to make the projects. They can be traced from the pages and used straight away. However, it may be that you love a particular motif and would like to incorporate it into another project and therefore need to enlarge it or make it smaller. Go to your local photocopying shop (or most grocery stores have photocopiers) and get them to do this for you.

The alphabet can be used to personalize projects; embroider with backstitch, working the dots with French knots.

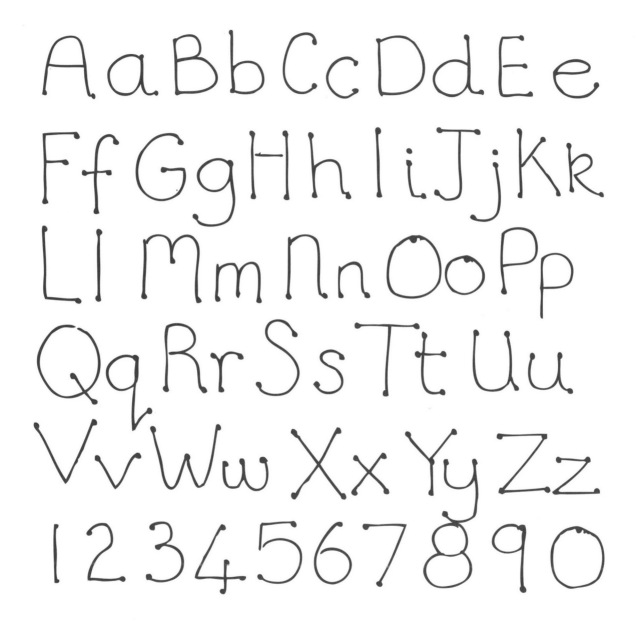

Aa Bb Cc Dd Ee
Ff Gg Hh Ii Jj Kk
Ll Mm Nn Oo Pp
Qq Rr Ss Tt Uu
Vv Ww Xx Yy Zz
1 2 3 4 5 6 7 8 9 0

Stacked Heart

random cross stitch
between hearts

infill chain
stitch

running stitch heart

backstitch heart

blanket stitch heart

chain stitch heart

alternate lazy daisy flowers and French knots between hearts

embroider a herringbone stitch border around the outer heart

note: the largest
heart is used as
the template for
the Heart Blanket

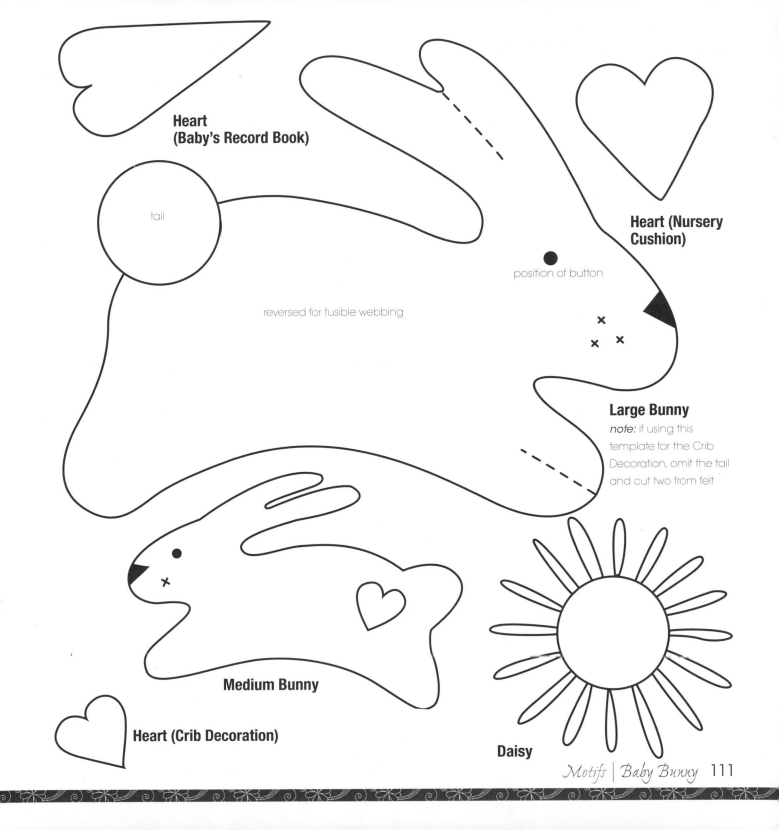

Heart (Baby's Record Book)

tail

reversed for fusible webbing

Heart (Nursery Cushion)

position of button

Large Bunny
note: if using this template for the Crib Decoration, omit the tail and cut two from felt

Medium Bunny

Heart (Crib Decoration)

Daisy

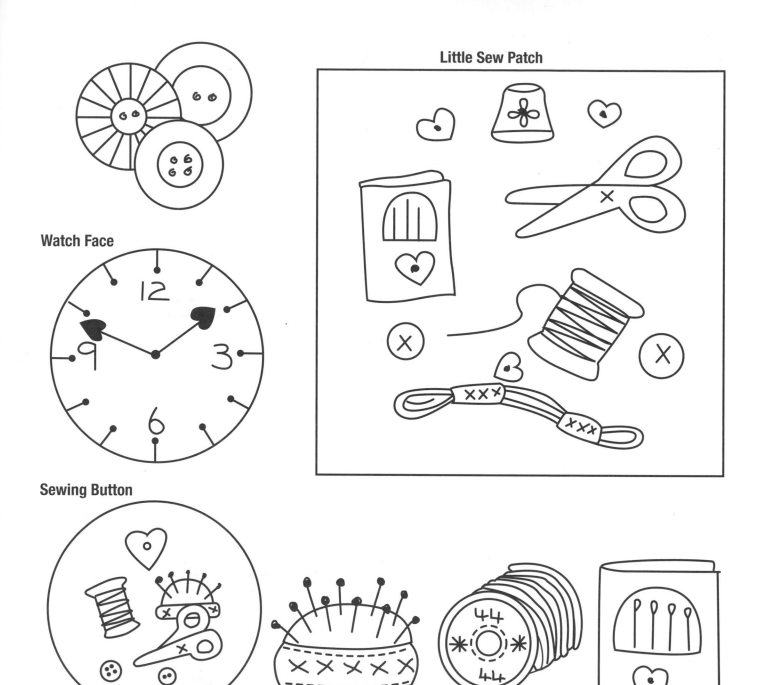

Little Sew Patch

Watch Face

Sewing Button

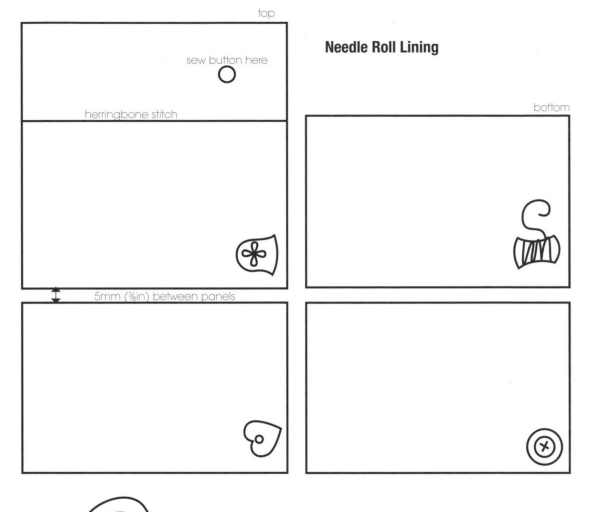

top

sew button here

Needle Roll Lining

bottom

herringbone stitch

5mm (⅜in) between panels

Cutlery Set

Large Jam Jar

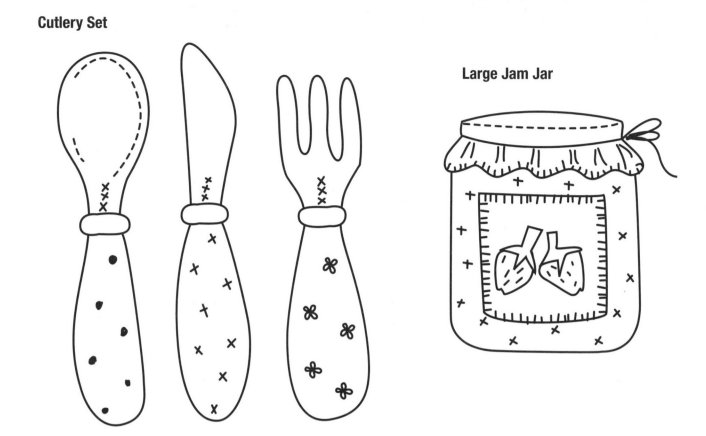

Cupcake

Small Jam Jar

Plate

note: all motifs on
these pages are used
on the Gardener's Tidy,
except for the Seed
Head opposite

Seed Head

Button Collage

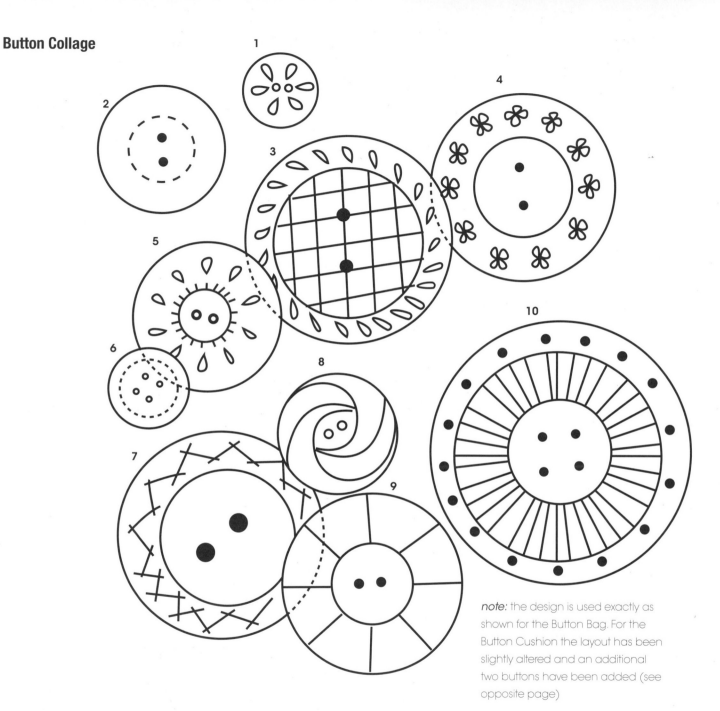

note: the design is used exactly as shown for the Button Bag. For the Button Cushion the layout has been slightly altered and an additional two buttons have been added (see opposite page)

1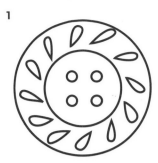

2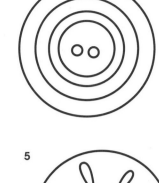

3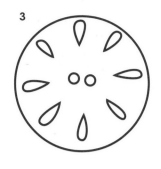

4

5

6

Button Cushion

note: additional buttons to be added to the Button Collage design

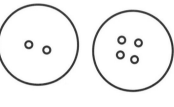

7

8

9

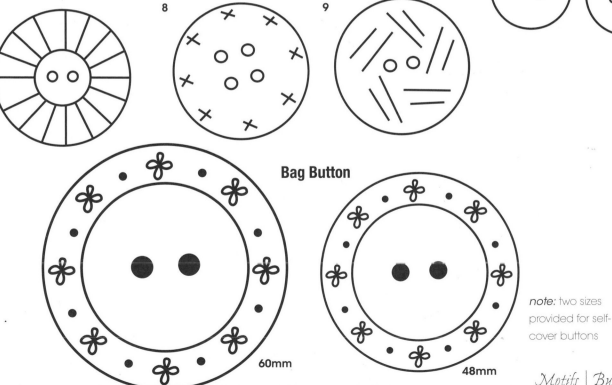

Bag Button

note: two sizes provided for self-cover buttons

60mm

48mm

Suitcase

Small Luggage Tag

sew button here

Eiffel Tower

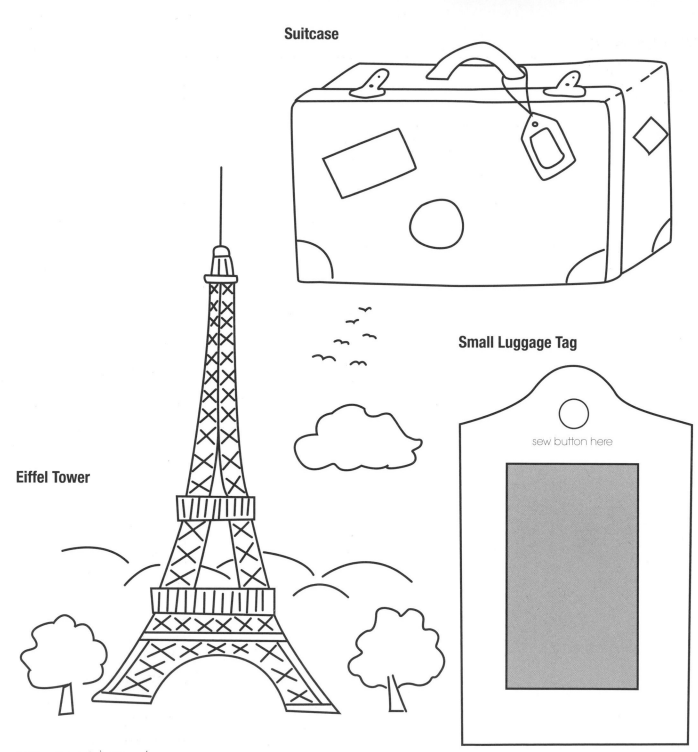

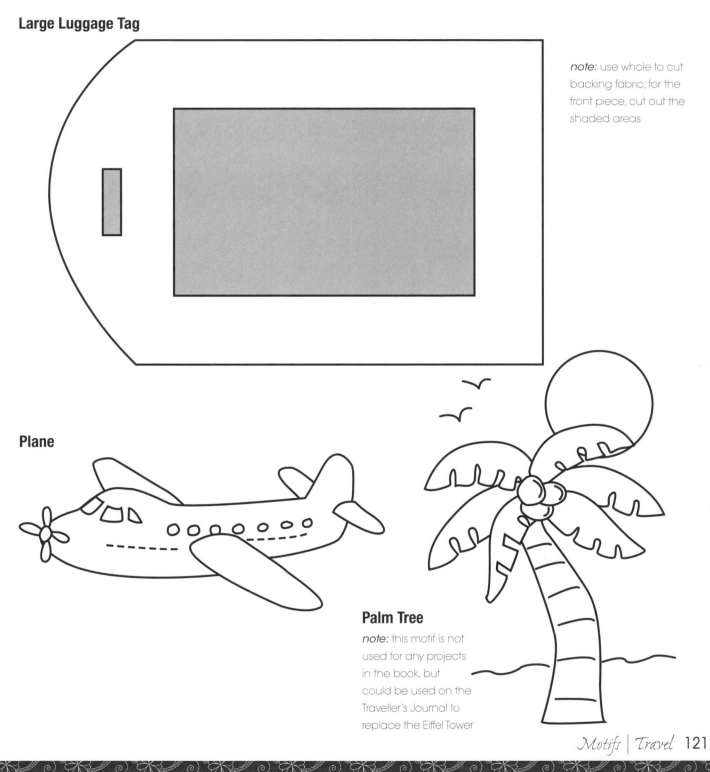

Large Luggage Tag

note: use whole to cut backing fabric; for the front piece, cut out the shaded areas

Plane

Palm Tree

note: this motif is not used for any projects in the book, but could be used on the Traveller's Journal to replace the Eiffel Tower

Motifs | Travel 121

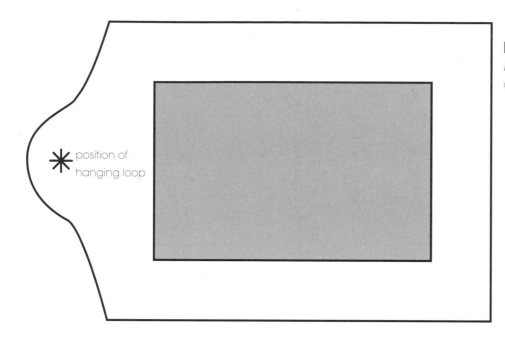

Present Tag

note: cut eight tags from red felt and cut out shaded area from four of the tags

Scene 1

Scene 2

Scene 3

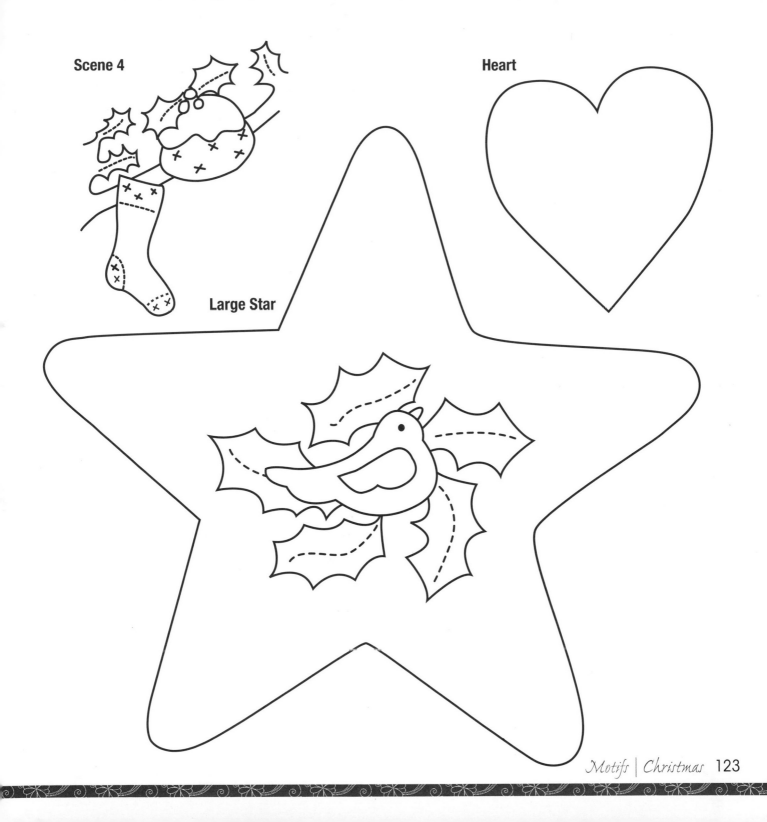

Scene 4

Heart

Large Star

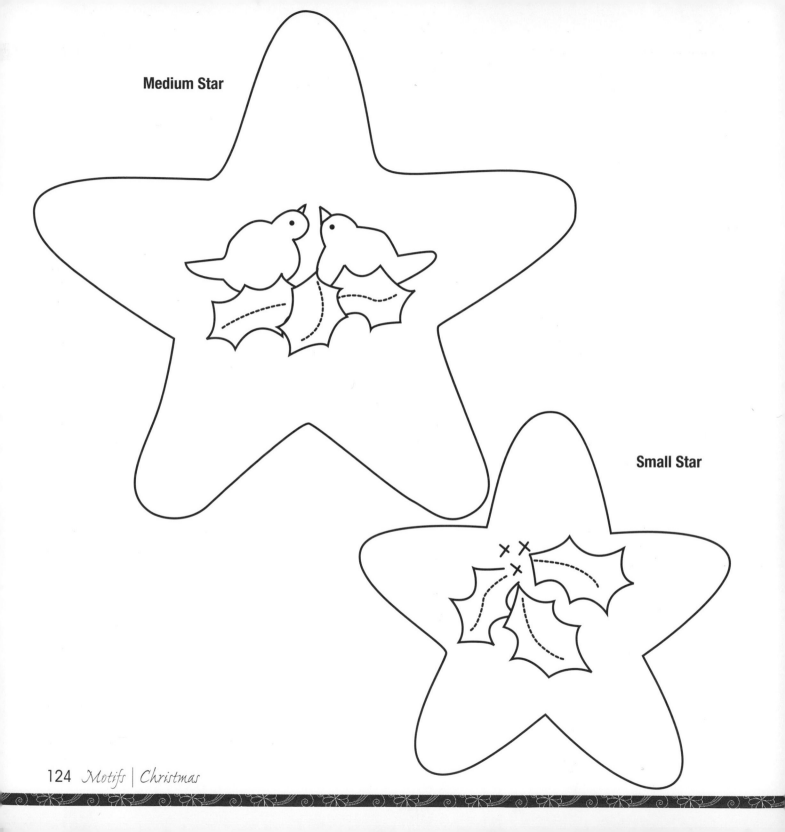

Medium Star

Small Star

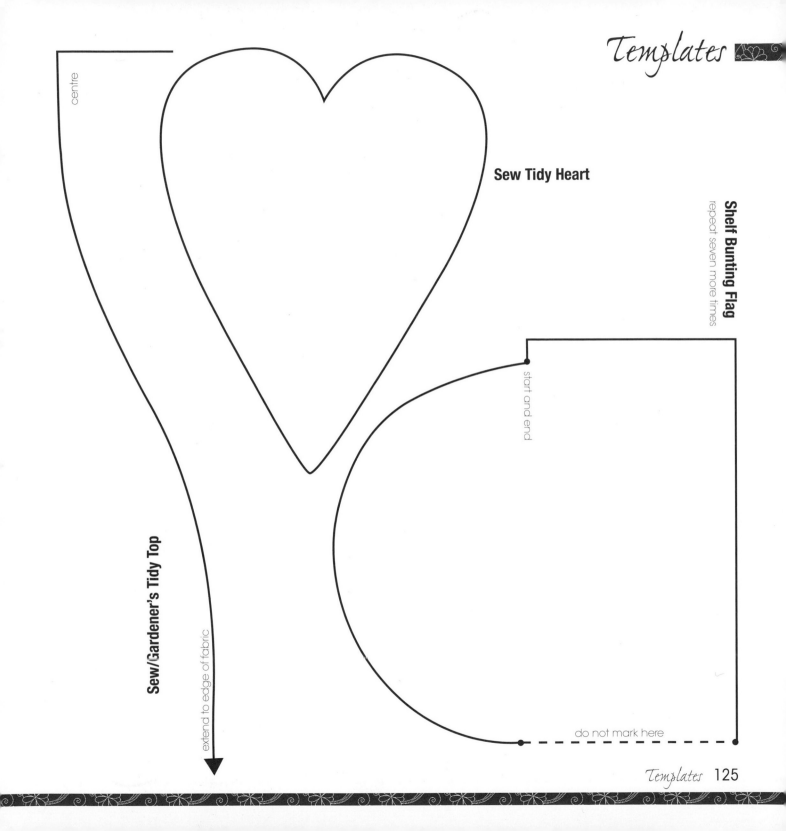

centre

Sew Tidy Heart

Shelf Bunting Flag
repeat seven more times

start and end

Sew/Gardener's Tidy Top

extend to edge of fabric

do not mark here

Acknowledgments

As always my greatest thanks go to those people who believe in me and encourage me all the way: Gill from the Patchwork Dog and Basket; the girls at David & Charles; the Tuesday, Wednesday and Thursday morning ladies – you are all very special, we have lost together but gained oh so many babies; Iris Primrose, Jenny and Maggie – thank you my lovelies. Also for my beautiful daughters, thank you. But extra special thanks and love must go to Harvey, my son, and Phil, my husband, who put up with me sewing in the car, at guitar lessons, on the football pitch, in a plane, at the beach, in bed, in the bathroom, in the garden, whilst cooking and often when eating – only you and I know this is not normal!

About the Author

Mandy Shaw lives with her husband and four children, dog, cat, tortoise, three fish and three chickens in the market town of Hailsham, East Sussex. Mandy's passion for needlework was nurtured at the local comprehensive by Miss Swift. After tackling most crafts she discovered patchwork and creative textiles, and she began designing and writing patterns for her own company, Dandelion Designs. She teaches and lectures around the United Kingdom and runs a website selling her wares, www.dandeliondesigns.co.uk. This is her second book with David & Charles.

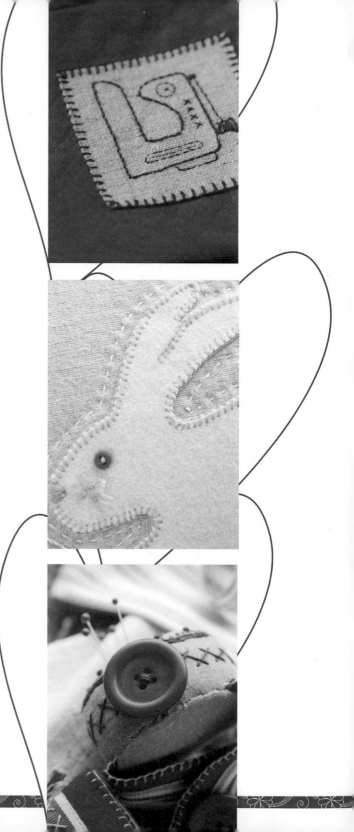

Suppliers

UK

Dandelion Designs

37 Summerheath Road, Hailsham,
East Sussex, BN27 3DS
www.dandeliondesigns.co.uk
*Supplier of Mandy's patterns and
kits and lots of fabric and haberdashery
items related to this book including
tapes, ric-rac, self-cover buttons, linens,
wool felt blanket, coton à broder and
other threads.*

The Patchwork Dog and Basket

The Needlemakers, West Street,
Lewes, East Sussex, BN27 2NZ
Tel: 01273 483886
www.patchworkdogandbasket.co.uk
*For patchwork and quilting fabrics,
buttons, tapes and haberdashery.*

Cowslip Workshops

Newhouse Farm, St Stephens,
Launceston, Cornwall, PL15 8JX
Tel: 01566 772654
www.cowslipworkshops.com
*For fabrics (especially linen), as well as
a beautiful venue for workshops.*

Daisy Chain Designs

Meadowsweet, Caldicotts Lane,
Lower Dicker, East Sussex, BN27 4BG
Tel: 01323 848894
www.daisychaindesigns.co.uk
For patterns, kits and haberdashery.

The Cotton Patch

1283-1285 Stratford Road,
Hall Green, Birmingham, B28 9AJ
Tel: 0121 702 2840
www.cottonpatch.co.uk
For patchwork and quilting supplies.

Dunelm Mill

Green Street, Radcliffe,
Manchester, M26 3ED
Tel: 0845 165 6565
www.dunelm-mill.com
For feather cushions and stuffing.

The Quilt Room

37–39 High Street, Dorking
Surrey, RH4 1AR
Tel: 01306 877307
www.thequiltroom.co.uk
For patchwork and quilting supplies.

USA

The City Quilter

157 West 24th Street,
New York, NY 1011
Tel: 212 807 0390
For patchwork and quilting supplies.

Connecting Threads

13118 NE 4th Street,
Vancouver, WA 98684
Tel: 1 800 574 6454
www.connectingthreads.com
For general needlework supplies.

JoAnn Stores Inc

5555 Darrow Road,
Hudson, OH 44236
Tel: 1 888 739 4120
www.joann.com
For needlework and quilting supplies.

The Craft Connection

21055 Front Street, PO Box 1088,
Onley, VA 23418
Tel: 1 888 204 4050
www.craftconn.com
For fabrics and needlework supplies.

Hancocks of Paducah

3841 Hinkleville Road,
Paducah, KY 42001
Tel: 1 800 845 8723
www.hancocks-paducah.com
For general needlework supplies.

eQuilter

5455 Spine Road, Suite E,
Boulder, CO 80301
Tel: 877 322 7423
www.equilter.com
For fabrics, patterns and threads.

EUROPE

Den Haan & Wagenmakers

Nieuwezijds Voorburgwal 97-99,
1012 RE Amsterdam, The Netherlands
www.dutchquilts.com
For Dutch reproduction fabrics.